spanish country kitchen

spanish country kitchen

traditional recipes for the home cook

Linda Tubby

photography by Martin Brigdale

RYLAND
PETERS
& SMALL

LONDON NEW YORK

Dedication

For Jennifer and Simon Alvaro Borja Andres Tubby – the Spanish faction of our family – with love.

First published in Great Britain in 2005
by Ryland Peters & Small
20–21 Jockey's Fields
London WC1R 4BW
www.rylandpeters.com

10 9 8 7 6 5 4 3 2 1

Text © Linda Tubby 2005
Design and photographs
© Ryland Peters & Small 2005

ISBN 1 84172 945 0

A catalogue record for this book
is available from the British Library.

Printed and bound in China

Senior Designer Steve Painter
Commissioning Editor Elsa Petersen-Schepelern
Production Patricia Harrington
Art Director Gabriella Le Grazie
Publishing Director Alison Starling

Food Stylist Linda Tubby
Prop Stylist Helen Trent
Indexer Hilary Bird

Author's Acknowledgements

Without my sister-in-law, this book would not have been possible – a heartfelt thanks for her knowledge and her company during much eating and drinking in Spain and all post requirements so expertly carried out.

A big thanks to Elsa – an editor in a million – so supportive and helpful. For her much 'fashing' and all her wordly wisdom.

Special thanks to Steve for such a beautifully designed book and for his support during its creation.

Martin – thank you so much for such great creative and edible photography and lovely scene-setting shots.

Helen for splendidly stylish propping.

Thanks to all who helped at Ryland Peters and Small, especially Gabriella Le Grazie for her enthusiasm and Alison Starling.

My friend Paul Gayler for so much support, endless encouragement and much advice on Spanish cooking.

Señora Maria Esther Montalbo Montero, Juan Ramon Sainz Pardo and Alicia Nuñez Montalbo for all their kindness and helpful advice in Spain.

Karen and Mike Rogers of Philglas & Swiggot wine merchants for their help and advice on Spanish wines and sherry.

Brindisa, especially Claire Roff for all her help and information.

Dan at Mortimer and Bennet for much helpful advice on produce. Phil, Gary and Eddie at Covent Garden Fish in Chiswick for my usual happy and yummy fish and advice. Andrew at Andreas Georghiou for splendid fresh produce. Rodney at Macken and Collins for meat and service with a smile. Phil at Theobroma for chocolate advice.

Jamie Cañella for advice on all things Spanish.

All family, friends and supporters, who helped in many ways. Jerry for techy help and meals when the candle burnt into the night. With love and thanks to my wonderful, creative sons, Dan and Ben, and my special Mam Lou Simpson, who still amazes me with all her snippets of information.

Notes

- All spoon measurements are level unless otherwise stated.

- All herbs are fresh, unless specified otherwise.

- Eggs are large unless otherwise specified. Uncooked or partly cooked eggs should not be served to the very old, frail, young children, pregnant women or those with compromised immune systems.

- Most ingredients will be available in larger supermarkets and delicatessens. Others are available in Spanish shops, on-line or by mail order (page 142).

contents

the spanish country kitchen

Spanish country cooking has its roots in peasant cuisines in which each region relied on seasonal and locally available raw materials. Almost everywhere, traditional cooking is a product of climate and ingredients, history and religion, good times and bad. In Spain, more than anywhere else, cuisine seems to be closely linked to its history and religion.

Wheat, the olive and the vine go back to Phoenician times, but it was the Romans who made these – together with their beloved garlic – into the staples of Spanish cooking. Soon Spain became one of the agricultural engines of the Empire – as it is today of modern Europe.

The Romans were toppled by the Visigoths, and they, in turn, by the Moors – Muslims from North Africa. It was the Moorish presence that had the greatest and most lasting effect on the Spanish kitchen.

During the time in which they ruled most of Spain, they introduced many foods now thought indigenously Spanish. Oranges and pomegranates, figs and apricots, aubergines and asparagus, almonds and pistachios, sugar and rice, saffron and cinnamon – and the use of nuts and dried fruits in dishes of vegetables, fish or meat.

The Moors arrived in the 8th century, and stayed for 800 years until defeated in 1492 by Isabella and Ferdinand and expelled from their last great stronghold of Granada.

These same rulers were responsible for two enormous changes in the Spanish kitchen. First, they dispatched Columbus on his voyage of discovery that would win untold gold and other riches from Central and South America. There were culinary riches too, in the form of ingredients such as tomatoes and peppers, chillies and chocolate, vanilla and corn, potatoes and beans – all still so much identified with the Spanish cooking of today.

The 'Catholic kings', as they were called, were also responsible for the Spanish Inquisition, when the Catholic Church spread its control across the country. The forced conversion or expulsion of the Jews also occurred in 1492, and in 1502 the same fate awaited any Moors who remained. The Spanish culinary emphasis on pork and shellfish – sometimes together – is said to go back to this time. People would ostentatiously consume these dishes in public, because everyone knew that no Jew or Muslim would touch them, therefore the eater must be Christian.

Catholicism also encouraged the Spanish passion for fish. The rule was 'fish on Fridays', for the 40 days of Lent, and for innumerable Saints' Days throughout the year. Fresh fish and shellfish came from every coast, even to Madrid in the middle of the country. And if you couldn't have fresh fish, you had *bacalao* (salt cod). Today, salt cod is more expensive than fresh fish, but remains perennially popular.

Though Spaniards do cook at home, city dwellers are social butterflies – snacking at tapas bars and eating out at restaurants and terrazas. In the country however, people necessarily have to cook at home in their own kitchens.

Though modern Spanish kitchens are now like kitchens anywhere, formerly they were like those in other parts of southern Europe. Ovens were the preserve of the village baker, and even when rural houses had brick or stone ovens, they were usually outside. (Understandable when you remember the searing heat of a Spanish summer.)

In many farmhouse kitchens, food was and still is cooked on top of the stove or over a special grill called a *parrillada*, often just outside the kitchen door, because of the heat. Grilled, fried and boiled dishes are the typical home-style recipes. Typically Spanish cooking utensils such as *ollas* (pots), iron paella pans and terracotta cazuelas are available outside Spain, but even if you don't have them, ordinary frying pans, casseroles and saucepans will do very well. I hope you enjoy the recipes in this book, as much as I have collecting them.

tapas and salads

*tapas, huevos, entradas
y ensaladas*

Variations of this recipe are found all over Spain. However, I found this version in a *tasca* (tapas bar) in a little backstreet off the Plaza del Sol in Old Madrid. There were mini cazuelas of gambas all lined up, ready to fry and serve spitting hot to hungry Madrileños during the evening's tapas crawl. Serve with a very cold fino sherry.

garlic prawns
gambas al ajillo

48 small uncooked prawns, about 600 g, shelled and deveined, with tail shell left on

4 tablespoons extra virgin olive oil

8 garlic cloves, peeled and bruised

6 small dried chillies

8 small fresh bay leaves

freshly squeezed juice of ½ lemon

sea salt

Alioli

5 garlic cloves, finely chopped

a large pinch of salt

100 ml extra virgin olive oil

2 teaspoons lemon juice, plus extra to taste

100 ml sunflower oil

fine sea salt and freshly ground white pepper

4 individual cazuelas (terracotta ramekins), 10–12 cm diameter, preheated in a hot oven

Serves 4

To make the alioli, pound the garlic and a large pinch of salt to a smooth, thick, creamy consistency with a mortar and pestle. Slowly drip in the olive oil, mixing with the pestle. Switch to a whisk and mix in the lemon juice, pepper and, little by little, half the sunflower oil. Add 1–2 teaspoons cold water and whisk well while adding the remaining 50 ml oil. The mixture will be very thick. Set aside for at least 30 minutes for the garlic to mellow, then add salt, pepper and extra lemon juice to taste.

To prepare the prawns, put on a plate and sprinkle lightly with salt. Heat the oil in a frying pan, add the garlic and fry until brown. Add the chillies, bay leaves and prawns all at once and fry without turning until the prawns are crusted and curled on one side, then turn them over and crust the other side, about 3½ minutes in total.

Transfer to the preheated cazuelas, sprinkle with lemon juice and top with a spoonful of alioli. Serve immediately while still bubbling hot.

Note Alioli, sometimes spelt 'allioli', is used with all sorts of dishes. Often an egg yolk is mixed in after the garlic is creamy, making it a little closer to the French aïoli. It's pungent yet delicious. When first made, it is quite strong, but after about 30 minutes the flavour really mellows. For an even milder taste, blanch the garlic cloves until just soft, then pop them out of their skins and pound to a cream.

Queso frito is a snack to be eaten hot, straight from the pan. It is made from Manchego, a sheep's cheese from La Mancha, which is either semi-cured, ripe or aged with a basket-weave-patterned rind in shades from the palest ochre to deep dark brown and black. Queso frito is one of the most popular tapas, perfect with manzanilla or fino sherry, or with Valdepeñas, a red wine from La Mancha. Sometimes, it is served with membrillo, Spanish quince paste. However, I like it best with a bowl of mixed green and black olives.

fried cheese
queso frito

275–300 g semi-cured Manchego cheese, 3 months old

2 tablespoons plain flour

1 egg, beaten

150 g lightly dried fine fresh white breadcrumbs

150 ml olive oil

a pinch of smoked sweet paprika (smoked pimentón dulce), to serve

To serve (optional)

membrillo (quince paste)

mixed olives

Serves 6

Cut all the rind off the Manchego and cut the cheese into 1 cm wedges.

Put the flour on a small plate and, working in batches of 6, dip each wedge in the flour, then in the beaten egg, then in the breadcrumbs.

Heat half the oil in a non-stick frying pan over medium heat, then fry the wedges in batches until golden – about 45 seconds each side. Drain on kitchen paper.

Wipe out the pan (to get rid of burnt breadcrumbs) and fry the remaining batches in the same way.

Sprinkle with a pinch of paprika and serve with membrillo or olives, if using.

Note Membrillo is a thick paste made from quinces, a golden fruit related to the apple and pear, available in autumn. Quinces are cooked into puddings, jellies or jams, and into this sweetly smoky paste. Membrillo is also served with a good Manchego cheese instead of pudding.

A tapa is a lid – and the original tapas were slices of bread or small plates put on top of a glass of sherry or wine by the barman. Soon, delicious foods were used to top the bread or plate, and now we have a huge and delectable range of appetizers served in bars and restaurants from Sydney to Stockholm to Seattle. However, there's nothing to beat the real thing – the best version of this classic I've ever tasted was in a convivial bar in Granada. Serve it very hot, with lots of napkins, cocktail sticks, a bowl of coarse sea salt and a copita or two of chilled manzanilla sherry.

potato fritters with chorizo
buñuelos de patatas con chorizo

500 g potatoes, peeled and cut lengthways into thick fingers

1 tablespoon self-raising flour

2 eggs, separated, plus 1 egg white

100 g chorizo, skinned and chopped into small pieces

sea salt and freshly ground black pepper

pure olive oil or sunflower oil, for deep-frying

Makes about 24

Boil the potatoes in a saucepan of salted water until soft, drain through a colander and cover with a cloth for about 5 minutes to let them dry out. Transfer to a bowl, mash in the flour and season with a little pepper. Mix in the egg yolks, then stir in the chorizo.

Put the egg whites in a separate bowl and whisk until soft peaks form. Fold into the mashed potatoes a little at a time.

Fill a saucepan or deep-fryer one-third full with oil, or to the manufacturer's recommended level. Heat to 180°C (355°F).

Working in batches of 6, take heaped teaspoons of the mixture and lower into the hot oil. Fry each batch for 3 minutes until evenly golden, turning them over halfway through (if they brown too quickly they will not have a good texture in the centre). Keep the oil temperature constant. As each batch is done, drain on kitchen paper and keep them warm in a preheated oven 180°C (350°F) Gas 4 until all have been cooked. Serve hot.

Serve on a cocktail stick with bowls of olives and pimientos de Padrón, if you can find them in a Spanish deli. Emparedados make a great snack served with a glass of draught beer or a good chilled Chardonnay from Penedès.

hot sandwiches
emparedados calientes

8 slices jamón serrano

12 thin slices of sweet chorizo, such as vela dulce from la Rioja

8 slices 3-day-old bread, crusts removed

2 tablespoons grated Manchego cheese

4 eggs, beaten

90 ml extra virgin olive oil

fine sea salt and freshly ground black pepper

To serve

olives

pimientos de Padrón (optional)

Serves 4: makes 16 pieces

Divide the ham and chorizo between 4 slices of bread, grind over some pepper and sprinkle the grated cheese on top of the chorizo, keeping it to the centre of the slices. Put the remaining slices of bread on top and press down firmly.

Put the beaten eggs, salt and pepper in a flat dish large enough to take 2 sandwiches at a time and dip the sandwiches in the mixture.

Heat half the oil in a non-stick frying pan large enough to take 2 sandwiches at a time, then fry on both sides over medium heat until crisp and golden, 3–3½ minutes each. Repeat with the remaining oil and remaining sandwiches. Cut into triangles, skewer on sticks and serve while hot with olives, and pimientos de Padrón, if using.

Note Pimientos de Padrón are tiny green peppers named after Padrón in Galicia – you sometimes find them for sale in Spanish shops. Simply sautéed in olive oil, then sprinkled with salt, you eat them off the stalk, leaving the seeds behind. Be warned – about one in six will be as hot as a chilli! Just as you build up confidence, one comes along and blows your head off.

To make them, heat 2 tablespoons virgin olive oil in a large frying pan. Working in batches, add 200 g fresh green pimientos de Padrón and fry, shaking the pan, until the skins develop white blisters and the green colour intensifies. Remove from the pan, pile onto a plate and sprinkle with salt.

Migas are a national treasure. They are an ancient and original peasant snack – simply bread sprinkled with salted water, then fried in lovely green olive oil. These are flavoured with jamón serrano, but plain ones are served in many ways – sometimes with grapes, or fried eggs, or even with hot chocolate. There are countless regional variations; these are from Extremadura, noted for fine pigs and excellent ham. If serving as a pre-dinner snack, try a Spanish sparkling Cava.

migas with jamón
migas de extremadura

200 g dry 2-day-old country bread, crusts removed

125 ml extra virgin olive oil

100 g jamón serrano or streaky bacon, cut into 5 mm pieces, or bacon lardons

3 garlic cloves, bruised with the back of a knife

1 fat dried red chilli, such as ñora or ancho, deseeded and finely chopped

coarse sea salt

Serves 4

Cut the bread into fingers, spread out on a tea towel, then spray or sprinkle lightly with water and a little salt. Wrap up in the towel and leave for 2 hours. Unwrap the cloth and break the bread into big pieces.

Heat 2 teaspoons of the oil in a frying pan, add the ham and fry until crisp. Drain on kitchen paper.

Wipe the pan clean and heat the remaining oil. Add the garlic, fry until golden, then remove and discard. Add all the breadcrumbs at once and stir-fry until evenly golden. Stir in the chilli and ham and serve very hot. Eat with your fingers or little spoons.

I tasted this as a *pincho* (bar snack) with a few *chatos* (little shots of red wine) in a lovely little bar near the opera house in Madrid – the salt cod with spinach was a taste revelation.

spanish omelette of spinach and salt cod
tortilla de espinacas y bacalao

100 g boneless salt cod, cut into cubes

100 ml olive oil

1 small onion, finely chopped

250 g potatoes, scrubbed and thinly sliced

6 eggs

125 g cooked spinach, from 250 g uncooked

freshly ground black pepper

a deep frying pan, 20 cm diameter,
with rounded sides

Makes 12 pieces

Prepare the salt cod as in the recipe on page 26. Alternatively, make your own salt cod (below). Using your fingers, break up into flakes.

Heat 80 ml of the oil in the frying pan, add the onion and potatoes and fry for about 10 minutes until softened but not coloured – turn them frequently to prevent sticking.

Lightly beat the eggs in a bowl with pepper. It usually isn't necessary to add salt because the fish is already salty. Mix in the spinach and flaked fish.

Pour the mixture into the pan, moving it with a spatula so it flows under and over the potatoes. Cook until set on the bottom – shake the pan as it cooks and loosen the sides a little with a spatula. When it has set and is pale golden, put a plate on top of the pan, turn it upside down, then slide the tortilla onto the plate. Put the remaining oil in the pan. When hot, slide the tortilla back into the pan, cooked side up. Cook until golden. Slide onto a board or plate and leave for a minute before slicing.

Note To make your own salt cod, sprinkle a non-reactive dish with 75 g rock salt and put a 200 g skinless cod fillet on top. Cover with another 75 g salt and chill for 12 hours. Wash off the salt and soak in water for about 2 hours, changing the water several times. This recipe produces an attractive white result – ordinary dried salt cod can be cream in colour.

According to Alicia Rios and Lourdes March in their book *The Heritage of Spanish Cooking*, this classic Spanish egg dish was named after the palace of La Flamenca in Aranjuez, the former spring residence of the Spanish kings. Others say it looks like the bright, swirling skirts of a flamenco dancer. Whatever the origin, the result is delicious and easy to make.

baked eggs
with ham and chorizo
huevos a la flamenca

4 tablespoons olive oil

1 onion, finely chopped

1 garlic clove, crushed

125 g cubed Spanish panceta or bacon lardons

8 tomatoes, skinned, deseeded and chopped

½ teaspoon sweet paprika (pimentón dulce)

1 tablespoon dry sherry

2 large roasted red peppers from a jar or tin, cut into cubes

12 asparagus tips, cooked

50 g peas, blanched

4 very fresh eggs

8 very thin slices of large chorizo, about 35 g

coarse sea salt and freshly ground black pepper

a large cazuela, about 20 cm diameter, or 4 small ones (optional)

Serves 4

Heat the oil in a frying pan with ovenproof handle, add the onion and garlic and fry over medium heat for about 7 minutes until soft and just starting to turn golden. Add the panceta and fry for 3 minutes. Add the tomatoes, paprika and sherry and cook for about 7 minutes until slightly thickened. Season with a little salt and pepper.

Fold the roasted peppers, asparagus and peas into the mixture. (If finishing in a cazuela, transfer the vegetables to the dish at this point.) Make 4 indentations in the mixture and break in the eggs, swirl the white part slightly and leave the yolks whole. Bake in a preheated oven at 200°C (400°F) Gas 6 for about 10 minutes until the eggs have just set.

Meanwhile heat a second small frying pan and dry-fry the chorizo slices on both sides until the oil runs out and the edges are slightly browned. Put on top of the dish and serve.

Note The Spanish method for seasoning a terracotta cazuela is to submerge it in water for 12 hours, then rub several peeled cloves of garlic over the unglazed base. When the juices have been absorbed into the terracotta, fill the cazuela with water and 100 ml vinegar and put on top of the stove with a heat-diffusing mat underneath. Bring slowly to the boil and simmer until the liquid is reduced to about 100 ml. Let cool, rinse with water and the cazuela is ready to use.

As in all hot countries, cooling salads are a feature of many Spanish meals, in restaurants and in people's homes, always served as a first course. The most common is either a simple mixture of lettuce and tomato, or the ubiquitous ensalada de San Isidro, which is not unlike a salade Niçoise, with eggs, tuna, onion and olives. This salad comes from Valencia, which gave its name to a variety of sweet orange. Choose a white wine made from the Albariño grape variety; it will have the zinginess to complement the oranges and enough sweetness to suit the red pepper.

orange and potato salad
ensalada valenciana

2 oranges

2 small red onions, cut into slivers

6 medium salad potatoes

1 small roasted red pepper from a jar, cut into thin strips

fine sea salt and freshly ground green peppercorns

Dressing

1 teaspoon sherry vinegar or red wine vinegar

3 tablespoons sunflower oil

2 teaspoons extra virgin olive oil

Serves 4

Remove skin and pith from the oranges and slice the flesh into rounds, keeping any juices for the dressing. Put the slices in a serving dish and add the slivered onions.

To make the dressing, put the collected juice from the oranges in a bowl, add the vinegar, salt and pepper and gradually whisk in the sunflower and olive oils.

Cook the potatoes in a saucepan of boiling salted water. When just soft, drain well, and as soon as they are cool enough, remove the skins and slice the flesh. While still warm, pour over the dressing. When the potatoes are cold, mix into the oranges and onions in the serving dish.

Just before serving, spread the strips of red pepper on top, then sprinkle with more crushed green peppercorns.

Note Spanish salads are usually undressed, so the table is set with little containers of salt, oil and vinegar, so you can dress it yourself. The order is important; first comes plenty of salt, then lots of oil to carry the salt evenly through the leaves or other ingredients and protect them from the vinegar, which is added last and very sparingly.

Xató, pronounced 'chay-toh', was originally a fishermen's salad. Salt cod, usually from Norway, was a staple in Catholic Europe, in the Caribbean and parts of America – interestingly all regions of the world with a plentiful supply of their own fish. It is widely available in Spanish and Italian delis, Oriental and Caribbean markets, and must be soaked before use to soften it and remove the salt.

The lettuce is traditionally soaked in the sauce for 1 hour, but I prefer it given less time. This is a simplified version of the sauce found in old cookbooks, but other versions use Salsa Romesco (page 111). Spanish salads usually aren't tossed until you dress them yourself at the table, but this is an exception to the rule. Try to find the great Basque white wine, Txomin Etxanis, with its briny mineral notes – it's excellent with salt cod.

200 g skinless, boneless salt cod (bacalao), or homemade salt cod (see note page 20)

1 escarole lettuce or curly endive, leaves separated and kept in cold water for 30 minutes until crisp

3 slightly green tomatoes, cored and cut into pieces

8 anchovy fillets

225 g jar of good-quality tuna in olive oil

12 green olives

12 black olives

Xató sauce

2 dried chillies, about 5 cm long, such as Spanish guindillas

4 tablespoons sherry vinegar

½ teaspoon salt

10 blanched almonds, lightly toasted in a dry frying pan and chopped

3 garlic cloves, finely chopped

125 ml extra virgin olive oil

Serves 6

salt cod and tuna salad
xató

To prepare the salt cod, soak it in cold water for 12–24 hours, changing the water every 4–5 hours. This softens the flesh and reduces the salt. Just before you are ready to use it, drain well.

To make the sauce, soak the chillies in boiling water for 15 minutes. Drain, deseed and chop coarsely. Put the chillies, vinegar, salt, almonds and garlic in a blender and pulse to a purée. With the motor running, gradually add the oil. Transfer to a bowl.

Shred the soaked salt cod with your fingers and add to the sauce. Chill for about 30 minutes, so the fish 'cooks' a little in the acidity of the dressing.

Drain the lettuce and pat dry. Add to the sauce and toss gently. Put the tomatoes, anchovies and tuna on top of the lettuce, add the olives and toss just before serving.

Cabrales from Asturias and Picón (or Picos de Europa) from Cantabria are outstanding Spanish blue cheeses, with blue veins that are said to be almost purple. They are made from a combination of goats', sheep's and cow's milk from animals grazing on the high pastures of the Picos mountains, in the north of Spain. The whole cheeses are salted, wrapped in leaves and matured in limestone caves.

Both are excellent served on their own or as part of a cheeseboard with a white wine such as Albariño.

salad of chicory leaves and blue cheese
ensalada de endibias al cabrales

200 g blue cheese, such as the Spanish Cabrales or Picón, or French Roquefort

6 tablespoons whipping or single cream

6 heads of chicory (Belgian endive or witloof) or other crisp lettuce

3 tablespoons shelled walnuts, toasted in a dry frying pan and roughly broken

¼ teaspoon hot paprika (pimentón picante)

Serves 4

Put 150 g of the blue cheese in a salad bowl, then add the cream little by little, mixing to a smooth sauce.

Trim the bases from the chicory. Either cut them in half lengthways or separate the leaves. Add to the bowl of dressing. Sprinkle with the toasted walnuts and crumble the remaining cheese over the top. Dust with paprika and serve.

Note Spanish paprika is available in three forms; pimentón dulce is mild and sweet, pimentón picante is hot and spicy, while pimentón agridulce is bitter-sweet. The smoked versions are made from chillies hung whole in traditional mud houses above oak fires that burn for 10–15 days. All are available in food shops or by mail order from sources on page 142.

This is a very fresh, sunny-day sort of salad with clean, crisp flavours. It contains the jewel-like seeds of the pomegranate, a fruit introduced to Spain by the Moors. Their name for it was *granada*, which means 'grain', referring to its hundreds of seeds, and they also named their great Andalusian city, Granada, after the pomegranate.

pomegranate salad with frisée leaves
ensalada granadina

1 frisée lettuce

1 large pomegranate or 2 small

100 g young carrots, sliced very finely on a mandoline

3 tablespoons virgin olive oil (see note)

4 garlic cloves, finely sliced

1 tablespoon moscatel or other white wine vinegar

coarse sea salt and freshly ground black pepper

serves 6

To make the frisée leaves crisp, separate the leaves, soak in a bowl of cold water for about 30 minutes, then drain and dry in a salad spinner. Break up the leaves into a serving bowl.

Working over a small bowl to catch the juices, open the pomegranate, separate the seeds and discard the skin and white pith – take care, because the juice stains. Sprinkle the seeds over the lettuce and add the carrot slices.

Put the oil and garlic in a frying pan, heat gently and fry until just golden. Remove the garlic with a slotted spoon and sprinkle over the leaves.

Add the vinegar to the bowl of pomegranate juices, then whisk in the olive oil from the frying pan. Add salt and pepper to taste and let cool for a few minutes. Pour the dressing over the salad and toss just before serving.

Note Extra virgin olive oil would be too strong for the sweet, slightly astringent juices of the pomegranate, so use virgin olive oil instead.

AQUI SE VENDEN
EMBUTIDOS
DE
Ca'n Tia

SOBRASADA DE CERDO
NEGRO

SOBRASADA CASERA
MALLORQUINA DE ARTA

Sobrasada y Longaniza
Caseras de Arta
750 pts Kg

Sobrasada y
Longaniza
Payesa Casera
750 Kg

RASADA · COLMADO STO. DOMINGO

FRUTAS 130

FRUTAS 80

FRUTAS 95

FRUTAS 70

FRUTAS 95

PERLAS DE CARLET

soups and two-course dishes
sopas y cocidas

Spaniards use garlic liberally in their cooking; it is prized for its fine flavour, of course, but also seen as good for the digestion and a cure for all ills. Traditional garlic soup is made with just bread, oil, garlic and water – healthy, simple food still loved all over Spain. I like to serve it with a poached egg on top, but you might like to try the other common variations listed below. A true, dry, aged amontillado sherry, with its distinctively nutty flavour, would be ideal to drink.

garlic soup
with poached egg
sopa de ajo al huevo escalfado

4 slices of bread from a long loaf

6 garlic cloves, lightly crushed but left whole

6 tablespoons olive oil

1 teaspoon sweet paprika (pimentón dulce), plus extra for sprinkling

1 teaspoon hot paprika (pimentón picante)

½ teaspoon ground cumin

1.25 litres clear chicken stock or half stock, half water

4–8 very fresh eggs

sea salt

4 individual ovenproof soup plates or bowls

a baking sheet

Serves 4

Rub the slices of bread with a garlic clove, brush with half the oil, then toast under a preheated moderate grill until golden. Put into the ovenproof soup plates and set them on the baking sheet.

Heat the rest of the oil in a shallow saucepan, add the garlic and fry until golden. Stir in both kinds of paprika and the cumin, then immediately add the stock and season with salt. Simmer for a few minutes, then pour over the bread. Break 1–2 eggs into the liquid in each plate and transfer to a preheated oven at 200°C (400°F) Gas 6 until the egg white has set but the yolk is still runny. Alternatively, poach the eggs separately and put on top of the toast, as shown here. Serve immediately, sprinkled with a little paprika.

Variations
• A version of this soup from Castile is made in a cazuela. The eggs are lightly beaten, then poured over the top. The cazuela is put under the grill and the eggs form a golden surface on the soup.
• In Madrid, they like to serve it with whole eggs broken in, then mixed to cook in the hot broth.

There are more than thirty variations of gazpacho, only some of which are the familiar raw, cold, tomato-based mixture. This version is typical of Andalusia in the hot south. Originally, it was a peasant dish that made use of the three basic ingredients much revered in Spain – oil, water and bread (in Arabic, *gazpacho* means 'soaked bread'). Other ingredients were added according to what was available. If you chill it, put it in a container with a tight-fitting lid so the flavours don't mingle with anything else in the refrigerator.

gazpacho

1 large sweet Spanish onion, finely chopped

1½ teaspoons caster sugar

4 tablespoons white wine vinegar

1 large red pepper, peeled with a vegetable peeler and coarsely chopped

1 large green pepper, peeled with a vegetable peeler and coarsely chopped

3 slices country-style bread, with crusts, about 100 g

3 garlic cloves, crushed

2.5 kg ripe tomatoes, skinned

12 cm cucumber, peeled and coarsely chopped

6 tablespoons virgin olive oil

fine sea salt

a splash of Tabasco (optional)

ice (optional)

Garnishes

6 cm cucumber, unpeeled, finely chopped

1 cm bread croutons, sautéed in olive oil infused with garlic

2 ripe tomatoes, finely chopped

Serves 6

Put one-quarter of the chopped onion in a small bowl and add ¼ teaspoon of the sugar, ½ teaspoon vinegar and 3 tablespoons cold water and set aside. Reserve one-quarter of the prepared red and green peppers and put in small bowls. These small bowls will be served as garnishes at the end.

To make the other garnishes, put the unpeeled chopped cucumber, croutons and chopped tomatoes in separate small bowls and set aside.

To make the gazpacho, put the bread, garlic and remaining sugar in a flat dish, sprinkle with the remaining vinegar and 250 ml cold water and let soak.

Cut the skinned tomatoes in half and cut out the hard core. Put a sieve over a bowl and deseed the tomatoes into the sieve. Push the seeds with a ladle to extract all the juices. Put the juices in a blender and discard the seeds. Add the soaked bread mixture and half the tomatoes. Blend until smooth and pour into a bowl.

Put the remaining tomatoes, the remaining onion and 100 ml iced water in the blender. Pulse 8 times to get a medium chunky effect, then pour into the bowl. Put the remaining chopped peppers, coarsely chopped cucumber, oil, salt and 150 ml iced water in the blender and pulse 8 times. Add to the bowl and stir in Tabasco, if using. Chill for up to 2 hours.

If you like ice added, serve with crushed ice cubes. Put the bowls of garnishes on the table for guests to scatter over the gazpacho.

White gazpacho is a pale and distinctively interesting version that certainly predates the tomato recipe. The Moors brought almonds to Spain about seven centuries before the arrival of tomatoes and peppers from the New World. The grapes are usually peeled, but if time is short just squash them a little to release their flavour. The gazpacho is generally served very cold, but cold grapes lose their flavour, so add them just before serving. Serve with a well-aged amontillado sherry.

chilled almond soup with grapes
gazpacho blanco con uvas

100 g blanched almonds

2 garlic cloves, crushed

3 slices of bread, crusts removed

3 tablespoons moscatel or other white wine vinegar

1 teaspoon salt

100 ml extra virgin olive oil

To serve

about 150 g assorted green and black grapes, peeled and deseeded

4 tablespoons extra virgin olive oil

Serves 4

Grind the almonds as finely as possible in an electric coffee grinder and put in a blender with the garlic, bread, vinegar and salt. Add 250 ml cold water, work to a purée, then, using the back of a ladle, push through a sieve set over a bowl.

Put the solids back in the blender with about 375 ml extra cold water, depending on the thickness required. With the motor running, gradually add the oil. Chill in the refrigerator for up to 2 hours.

Pour into 4 chilled soup bowls, add the grapes and drizzle 1 tablespoon extra virgin olive oil over each serving.

Note Serve as a starter, or in small glasses for a picnic or a party.

Aranjuez, just south of Madrid, is famous for its royal palace, its beautiful gardens, strawberries and asparagus. In April, the street stalls are piled high with huge bundles of fat and thin, wonderfully bright green asparagus as well as the fat white variety so popular in mainland Europe. Soups go well with sherry – try a manzanilla with this dish.

cream of asparagus soup
crema de espárragos

750 g asparagus
3 tablespoons olive oil
1 tablespoon butter
2 leeks, well washed and thinly sliced
1 onion, finely chopped
1 litre chicken stock
freshly grated nutmeg
150 ml double cream
fine sea salt and freshly ground white pepper

Serves 4

Cut the tips off 8 asparagus spears and reserve. Chop the remainder into 2 cm pieces.

Heat the oil and butter in a saucepan, add the leeks and onion, cover and sauté over gentle heat for 10 minutes. Add the chopped asparagus, stock, grated nutmeg, season well with salt and pepper and simmer for 10 minutes.

Transfer to a blender, purée until smooth, then, using the back of a ladle, push through a sieve set over a bowl. Alternatively, use a mouli. Add two-thirds of the cream to the bowl and stir well. Return the soup to the saucepan and heat gently when ready to serve (do not let boil).

Cook the reserved asparagus tips in boiling water until just tender. Ladle the soup into bowls, spoon the remaining cream on top, add the asparagus tips and some more nutmeg, then serve.

In all traditional Spanish recipes, there are many variations on a theme: this is no exception. Often the soup has just bread to thicken the liquid, but this version uses *fideos* (Spanish noodles). I have used a mixture of pork and veal to make the meatballs, but it would be fine to use just pork.

Try a typical red wine from Catalonia, such as Priorat – dark, almost inky black. Alternatively, seek out wines from neighbouring Montsant, made with the Spanish version of the French Grenache grape, Garnacha.

catalan meatball soup
sopa de albondiguillas catalana

1.2 litres chicken stock

2 tablespoons tomato purée

4 tomatoes, skinned, deseeded and finely chopped

30 g fideos, a double handful (see note)

fine sea salt and freshly ground white pepper

mint leaves, to serve

meatballs

150 g minced pork

150 g minced veal

1 small onion, grated

1 garlic clove, crushed

1 egg, beaten

1 tablespoon chopped fresh mint

2 tablespoons chopped fresh parsley

1 tablespoon fine freshly made breadcrumbs

a pinch of cinnamon

sea salt and freshly ground black pepper

plain flour, for dusting

2 tablespoons olive oil, for frying

Serves 4–6

To make the meatballs, put the pork and veal mince in a bowl with the grated onion, garlic, egg, chopped mint and half the chopped parsley. Mix in the breadcrumbs, cinnamon, salt and pepper. Using your hands, mix to a paste and form into 1.5 cm balls. Toss in flour until lightly coated.

Heat the oil in a frying pan and fry the balls over high heat to give a little colour and to firm them up a little.

To make the soup, put the stock in a large saucepan and bring to the boil. Add the tomato purée, tomatoes, fideos noodles, salt and pepper.

Add the meatballs to the pan and simmer gently for 5 minutes. Stir in the remaining parsley and serve with the mint leaves on top.

Note In Catalonia, the regional name for *fideos* is *fideus*. If you can't find this Spanish pasta, buy the broken vermicelli sold in Jewish delis for making chicken soup.

This meal-in-a-pot forms the classic family feast beloved of all Spaniards, rich or poor, in every region. It is known by different names in each area, but is essentially the same dish. It comes in two parts; first you eat the broth with the noodles, then the meat and sausages, with the vegetables and chickpeas. Set the table with large soup bowls at each place.

el cocido

250 g dried chickpeas

2 teaspoons salt, plus extra for the cabbage

750 g beef brisket, rolled

500 g piece of belly pork, without skin and bones

500 g piece of smoked back bacon or shoulder

2 whole chicken legs

2 fresh bay leaves

2 small onions

6 small carrots

a bunch of small turnips

a bunch of flat leaf parsley, tied together

2 sweet chorizos (chorizo dulce)

2 morcilla, Spanish salchicha or Italian fresh pork sausages (optional)

500 g new potatoes

1 small Savoy cabbage

2 tablespoons extra virgin olive oil

2 garlic cloves, bashed until bruised and split

100 g fideos or fine vermicelli noodles

pickled mild green chillies, to serve

a large piece of muslin

Serves 6-8

The day before you want to serve the cocido, put the chickpeas in a bowl, cover well with cold water, mix in 2 teaspoons salt and leave overnight.

Also the day before, put the beef, belly pork, bacon, chicken legs and bay leaves in a large saucepan or stockpot. Add cold water to cover by 3 cm. Bring slowly to the boil and simmer gently for 45 minutes. Remove the chicken legs (put in a bowl, cool, cover and chill). Continue cooking the other meats for 30 minutes. Transfer to a bowl, let cool, then chill. The next day, skim the fat off the meat.

Drain the chickpeas and put in a saucepan with cold water to cover by 2 cm, bring to a rapid boil and, when the froth rises, add a cup of cold water and skim. Repeat once more, then simmer for 15 minutes. Drain the chickpeas through a colander lined with muslin. Put one of the onions on top, then tie up the muslin into a bag.

Put the bag of chickpeas in a large stockpot, then add the cooked beef, pork and bacon, the other onion, carrots, turnips, parsley and stock. Slowly bring to a very gentle simmer, then continue simmering for 30 minutes.

Meanwhile, bring a second saucepan of water to the boil, add the chorizos and morcilla or pork sausages and blanch for 5 minutes over low heat. Drain and add to the meats. Add the potatoes to the meats and cook everything on a very low heat for a further 30–45 minutes. Add the chicken for the last 20 minutes. Check to make sure everything is tender.

Cut the cabbage into 2.5 cm pieces, cook in a saucepan of boiling salted water for 5 minutes, then drain. Heat the oil in a frying pan and fry the garlic until just golden, then remove the garlic, add the cabbage and fry for 2 minutes.

Remove 1.2 litres of stock from the meats, transfer to a saucepan, add the fideos, bring to the boil, cook for 5 minutes, then pour into a tureen to serve.

Cut up the meats and sausages and put them on a serving platter. Take the meat off the chicken and add to the platter. Add the turnips and carrots. Put the chickpeas on a second plate and add the cabbage. Put everything on the table and let everyone help themselves.

rice, pasta and savoury pies
arroz, pastas y masa

A two-course dish of rice and fish. The rice is cooked in a rich stock, then the fish and shellfish are eaten with pungently flavoured salsas (or you can just eat everything together). In Valencia and Alicante, this is just as popular as the better-known seafood paella.

rice 'apart' with seafood
arroz abanda

750 g halibut fillets

12 medium unshelled prawns

4 langoustines (scampi), or extra prawns

500 g clams

3 tablespoons olive oil

1 medium onion, finely chopped

2 garlic cloves, finely chopped

5 tomatoes, skinned, deseeded and finely chopped

375 ml measured Spanish rice, such as bomba or paella rice

coarse sea salt and freshly ground black pepper

Stock

1 tablespoon olive oil

1 medium onion, finely chopped

1 garlic clove, finely chopped

2 tomatoes, coarsely chopped

2–3 fish frames and 1 fish head (from the fishmonger)

a pinch of saffron threads, toasted in a dry frying pan, then crushed

3 bay leaves

3 sprigs parsley

coarse sea salt and freshly ground black pepper

To serve

Salsa Salmoretta (page 91) or Salsa Romesco (page 111)

Alioli (page 11)

a paella pan

kitchen foil

Serves 4

To prepare the fish and seafood, cut the halibut into 5 cm pieces and season lightly with salt and pepper. Shell and devein the prawns, leaving the tail fin on. Reserve the heads and shells.

Put 400 ml cold water in a saucepan and bring to the boil. Add a pinch of salt and cook the prawns and langoustines for 2 minutes. Remove with a slotted spoon and transfer to a bowl. Return the water to the boil, add the clams, cover and cook for 1½ minutes until they open. Strain through a colander over a bowl, reserving the liquid. Rinse the clams briefly under the cold tap to stop them cooking, then add to the prawns and langoustines.

To make the stock, heat the 1 tablespoon oil in a saucepan, add the onion and garlic and fry until softened. Add the 2 tomatoes, then cook for 3 minutes over medium heat. Add the fish bones and head, prawn heads and shells, saffron, bay leaves, parsley, salt, pepper and 800 ml cold water. Slowly bring to the boil, lower the heat and simmer for 25 minutes. Strain through a fine-meshed sieve.

Meanwhile, heat a paella pan or a large frying pan with ovenproof handle, add the 3 tablespoons oil, onion and garlic. Fry until golden. Add the 5 tomatoes and cook until they soften to a sauce. Stir in the rice and 500 ml of the stock. Season with salt and pepper and simmer for 3 minutes. Transfer to a preheated oven and cook at 200°C (400°F) Gas 6 for 10 minutes. Add 200 ml of the clam liquid and cook for a further 5 minutes. Remove from the oven and keep warm.

Put the remaining clam liquid and remaining fish stock in an ovenproof dish, add the halibut, cover and cook in the oven for 5 minutes. Turn the oven off. Add the seafood to the halibut and cover with foil. Loosely cover the rice with foil and put both foil-covered dishes back in the oven for a further 5 minutes. Transfer the rice to a serving dish and the fish and seafood to a separate platter.

Serve the rice first, followed by the seafood with salsa salmoretta or romesco and alioli.

4 tablespoons olive oil

3 chicken breasts with skin, cut into 4 pieces each

2 skinless duck breasts, cut into 5 pieces each

1 red pepper, deseeded and cut into long chunks

2 small hot (picante) chorizos, skin removed, flesh cut into 1.5 cm slices

2 tomatoes, skinned, deseeded and chopped

1 teaspoon sweet paprika (pimentón dulce)

a large pinch of saffron

2 sprigs of rosemary

1.1 litres clear chicken stock or water

150 g thin green beans

150 g shelled broad beans (optional), from 500 g with pods

100 g cooked white Spanish beans (alubias), butter beans or haricots

150 g shelled peas

300 g bomba or other short grain paella rice (do not wash)

coarse sea salt

1 onion, cut into wedges, soaked in cold water for 5 minutes, to serve

a paella pan

Serves 4–6

The Albufera in the Valencia region is a large lagoon where the Moors planted rice in the 8th century. The fertile land beyond, known as *huertas* (gardens), offered all the goodies necessary to make this original paella. People used what was available from the land, not the sea (that version came later), such as rabbit, duck, snails, eels, vegetables, herbs and rice.

The pan is crucial to the success of paella: it should be wide and shallow with two handles, ideal for the traditional method of cooking over an open fire. Cooked this way, a golden crust forms on the bottom and sides: this is called *socarrat* and is much prized.

Serve with an Albariño or an oaky Chardonnay.

traditional chicken paella
paella valenciana de la huerta

Heat the oil in a paella pan set over 2 burners or over a preheated barbecue. Add the chicken and duck and fry on all sides until golden. Halfway through cooking, add the red pepper and chorizos. Add the tomatoes, paprika, saffron, rosemary, and salt, then pour in all the stock. Bring to the boil, then lower the flame so it simmers very gently for 15 minutes.

Add the green and white beans and the peas. Pour in the rice (traditionally in the form of a cross). Mix into the stock – do not stir again. Let cook over low heat for another 15 minutes.

Increase the heat to high for 1 minute – this creates the socarrat if you aren't cooking the paella over an open fire.

Remove from the heat and leave for 5–10 minutes before serving with raw onion wedges. (It is important to serve it warm, not hot.)

This vegetarian dish comes from Valencia, where it is served during the Lenten fast. Its Spanish name means 'with partridge' – though the partridge is really a whole bulb of garlic. I like to use bomba rice, especially a brand called La Perdiz, with a drawing of a little partridge on its smart cloth cook (page 46). It is also good for soups, because the grains stay firm. Another wonderful variety is Calasparra rice from Murcia, just south of Valencia. Sold in numbered cotton bags, it is the best Spanish rice available. This kind of rice absorbs liquid without turning sticky, but there are rules – never wash it and stir it only once. Bomba will absorb double its own volume of liquid and the Calasparra up to three or four times.

baked rice with garlic
arroz al horno con perdiz

100 ml olive oil

1 whole head of garlic

1 large onion, finely chopped

4 tomatoes, skinned, deseeded and chopped (keep the juices)

1 teaspoon sweet paprika (pimentón dulce)

2 cups round grain rice, such as bomba

up to 1 litre vegetable stock or water

400 g canned chickpeas, rinsed and drained

50 g raisins, soaked in hot water for 30 minutes until plump

sea salt and freshly ground black pepper

a paella pan, cazuela or other ovenproof pan, 20–25 cm diameter

kitchen foil (optional)

Serves 6

Heat the oil in a paella pan, heatproof cazuela, heatproof shallow casserole or a frying pan with ovenproof handle. Add the garlic head and onion and fry for 12 minutes over low heat until the garlic is pale golden and beginning to soften and the onion soft and golden.

Remove the garlic and reserve. Increase the heat and add the tomatoes and juices. Cook until the mixture starts to thicken a little. Stir in the paprika, salt and pepper.

Stir in the rice. Add half the stock or water and bring slowly to the boil. Add the chickpeas, drain the raisins and gently fold them into the rice. Put the garlic in the centre and bake in a preheated oven at 180°C (350°F) Gas 4 for 10 minutes. Heat the remaining stock or water, then add as much as the rice seems to need. Continue baking for 10–15 minutes before serving, covering the top with foil if it seems to be over-browning or drying out. Serve from the pan.

The Moors introduced pasta to Catalonia in the form of *fideus* or *fideos* – short, thin pasta pieces, like Jewish vermicelli. The cooking methods for this dish bring together the two cornerstones of Catalan cooking. The first, *sofregit*, called *sofrito* elsewhere in Spain, is the basis for many dishes and sauces. In essence, it is lightly fried garlic and onions, with tomatoes and various other additions. The second is *picada*, a crushed mixture of fried bread, garlic, nuts and herbs, moistened and used as flavouring and thickener.

4 tablespoons olive oil

350 g pork spareribs, chopped into 4 cm pieces, then sprinkled with salt

200 g fresh spicy pork sausages (not chorizo), cut into 2 cm lengths

250 g fideos pasta or Jewish vermicelli

600 ml chicken stock, preferably homemade

sea salt and freshly ground black pepper

Sofregit (sofrito)

4 tablespoons olive oil

2 medium onions, finely chopped

1 garlic clove, finely chopped

4 tomatoes, skinned, deseeded and chopped

½ teaspoon sweet paprika (pimentón dulce)

Picada

1 thick slice of country bread, fried in olive oil

1 garlic clove, chopped

40 g pine nuts, lightly toasted in a dry frying pan

3 tablespoons finely chopped flat leaf parsley

a paella pan, shallow casserole or other ovenproof pan, 20–25 cm diameter

Serves 4

catalan pasta
fideus a la catalana

Heat 1 tablespoon of the oil in a paella pan, shallow heatproof casserole or frying pan with ovenproof handle. Add the spareribs and sausages, fry for 3 minutes on each side, then transfer to a plate. Wipe the pan clean and heat the remaining 3 tablespoons of the oil, add the pasta and fry over high heat for about 4 minutes until evenly golden. Transfer to a bowl.

To make the sofregit, heat the 4 tablespoons oil in the same pan, add the onions and garlic and fry for 5 minutes over low heat. Increase the heat, add the tomatoes, then cook for about 3 minutes until thickened. Stir in the paprika.

Add the ribs and sausages and push them down into the tomatoes, add the stock, salt and pepper and bring to the boil. Fold in the crisp pasta.

Bake in a preheated oven at 190°C (375°F) Gas 5 for 5 minutes. Stir in 400 ml boiling water and return to the oven for another 5 minutes. Push the crisp noodles from the top under the liquid and bake for another 10 minutes.

Meanwhile, to make the picada, cut the fried bread into pieces and put in a small processor with the garlic, pine nuts and parsley, and pulse to form a paste. Loosen with about 4 tablespoons boiling water, then fold into the pan of pasta.

Set the pan under a preheated grill about 20 cm from the heat for about 5 minutes just to crisp the top a little (don't let it burn). Serve from the pan.

2 tablespoons olive oil

1 large onion, finely chopped

2 garlic cloves, crushed

500 g skinless chicken breast, cut into 2.5 cm pieces

4 tablespoons dry white wine

3 tomatoes, skinned and chopped, reserving any juices

125 g chorizo, cut into thick slices

about 3 tablespoons chopped fresh oregano

½ teaspoon hot paprika (pimentón picante)

4 roasted red piquillo peppers, from a jar, coarsely chopped

2 tablespoons chopped fresh flat leaf parsley

4 hard-boiled eggs, shelled

coarse sea salt and freshly ground black pepper

Pastry

450 g plain flour, plus extra for kneading

75 g fine cornmeal

1 sachet fast-action dried yeast

1½ teaspoons fine sea salt

3 tablespoons butter or lard

200 ml milk

2 eggs

1 egg, beaten with 1 tablespoon water, for glazing

a baking tin with shallow sides, 32 x 22 cm, greased

kitchen foil (optional)

Makes 8 slices

There are many methods and combinations of ingredients used to make *masa de empanada*, the dough for covered pies. This version is from Galicia in north-west Spain – in other regions, such pies are called *pasteles*. Always hearty and delicious, they can have all kinds of fillings, such as spinach, pork and peppers or sardines and tuna. They are perfect for picnics, and deserve a good, robust red wine.

spicy chicken empanada
empanada gallega

Heat the oil in a flameproof casserole, add the onion and garlic and fry over medium heat for 5 minutes until softened but not coloured. Increase the heat and stir in the chicken, moving it around until it turns opaque. Add the wine, the tomatoes and their juices and cook until the sauce starts to thicken and the chicken has almost cooked.

Stir in the chorizo, oregano and paprika and season with salt and pepper. Transfer to a bowl and let the mixture cool completely.

To make the pastry, mix the flour, cornmeal, yeast and salt in a bowl. Put the butter and milk in a saucepan and heat until the butter has melted. When the milk has cooled a little to lukewarm, beat the 2 eggs in a bowl and stir in the milk.

Make a hollow in the flour and pour in the milk mixture. Mix with your hands to bring together into a ball. Transfer to a floured work surface and knead for about 5 minutes or until smooth and elastic. Put the dough in a lightly oiled bowl, cover with oiled clingfilm and set aside in a warm place until almost doubled in size.

Cut the dough in half and cover one piece. Roll out the other piece to the size of the baking tin, leaving a 2 cm overhang all round. Put into the tin and press into the angles. Stir the peppers and parsley into the cold filling, then spoon it evenly over the dough. Cut the hard-boiled eggs in half lengthways and nestle them into the filling.

Roll out the rest of the dough to fit the tin and carefully drape over the top. Brush egg wash around the edges of the overhanging pastry. Bring the pastry overhang up over the top pastry and crimp a little to seal. Brush all over with the remaining egg wash, make a few slits in the top with a knife or scissors and bake in a preheated oven at 180°C (350°F) Gas 4 for 30 minutes until golden and cooked (if over-browning, cover with foil). Serve hot or cold, cut into squares.

A *coca* is an open empanada, a bit like a pizza, that originates in Catalonia and the Balearics. It is cooked in communal outdoor stone or brick ovens. There are also thicker, sweet versions, with egg-enriched dough – good for breakfast or mid-morning snacks, and popular on particular saints' days. Authentically, a typical coca has just one or two topping ingredients. These days, anything goes – so, joining in with the spirit of things, I have added a few extra toppings to my moderately authentic coca. Serve with an easy-drinking, medium-bodied, soft red made from the Tempranillo grape, such as Rioja.

spanish flatbread
coca mallorquina

300 g strong white bread flour, plus extra for kneading

1 sachet easy-blend dried yeast

a pinch of sugar

1½ teaspoons fine sea salt

2 teaspoons olive oil

Topping

2 garlic cloves, crushed to a paste with salt

4 large tomatoes, core cut out with a small sharp knife and the flesh very finely sliced

2 courgettes, finely sliced on a mandolin

4 tablespoons pine nuts

5 tablespoons extra virgin olive oil

16 black olives

sea salt and freshly ground black pepper

1–2 baking sheets, oiled

Makes 2: serves 2–4

Put the flour in a bowl and mix in the yeast, sugar and salt. Make a hollow in the centre.

Put 250 ml hand-hot water in a bowl and mix in the oil. Pour into the hollow in the flour, then mix with your hands until the dough comes away from the bowl. If it seems too dry, add a little more water, about 1 tablespoon. Transfer to a lightly floured surface and knead for 5 minutes until smooth.

Put the ball of dough in an oiled bowl, cover with oiled clingfilm and set aside in a warm place for about 1 hour or until doubled in size.

Using a knife, cut half the dough out of the bowl and re-cover the bowl. Put the dough on a lightly floured work surface and knead to a flattened ball. Using a floured rolling pin, roll out to a rectangle about 30 x 20 cm x 5 mm thick. Transfer to an oiled baking sheet and roll up the edge a little to make a border.

To make the topping, mix the crushed garlic with 1 tablespoon of oil and smear half the mixture over the dough. Put half the tomato and courgette slices on top, sprinkle with half the pine nuts, salt and pepper, then drizzle with 2 tablespoons of the olive oil. Bake in a preheated oven at 220°C (425°F) Gas 7 for 10 minutes. Dot with half the olives and return to the oven for about 5 minutes or until golden and cooked.

Repeat with the other piece of dough and the remaining topping ingredients.

fish and seafood
pescados y mariscos

A classic dish from Santiago de Compostella, inland from the Atlantic coast of Galicia, where scallops grow in abundance. Santiago (St James) is the patron saint of Spain and the scallop shell is his emblem. For over a thousand years, pilgrims have made the long, arduous journey to this shrine, and in former times used scallop shells to scoop water from the streams. Today, the town is festooned with strings of shells painted with the sword of St James (page 137). The French scallop dish, Coquilles St Jacques, is named after the same saint. If you don't have scallop shells for this recipe, use small gratin dishes instead.

baked scallops
vieiras al gallego

6 large scallops

4 tablespoons extra virgin olive oil

1 medium onion, very finely chopped

1 garlic clove, finely chopped

1 medium-hot dried chilli, such as guindilla, deseeded and finely crushed

½ teaspoon sweet paprika (pimentón dulce)

250 g tomatoes, deseeded and finely chopped

1 tablespoon brandy

30 g fine fresh breadcrumbs

2 tablespoons finely chopped fresh flat leaf parsley

sea salt

4 large scallop shells or small gratin dishes

Serves 4

Cut the scallops in half horizontally and arrange 3 halves in each scallop shell or gratin dish. Season lightly.

Heat 2 tablespoons of the oil in a frying pan, add the onion and garlic and fry until very soft but not coloured. Stir in the chilli, paprika and tomatoes and cook for 3 minutes over medium heat. Add the brandy and continue cooking until thickened.

Mix the breadcrumbs with the parsley and a little salt. Spoon an equal amount of sauce over each scallop dish and sprinkle with the breadcrumb mixture. Spoon over the remaining oil and bake under a medium-hot grill for 5 minutes until golden. Serve at once.

Note One of the leading white wine varieties of Spain is Albariño, a favourite in trendy tapas bars from Barcelona to Madrid. It comes from the Rías Baixas region on the Atlantic coast between Santiago and the Portuguese border. Excellent, dry and aromatic, it is a great partner for all kinds of seafood.

I use small squid for this recipe. Even smaller ones, calamaritos, are only 2 cm long and are delicious fried in a light batter to serve as a tapa. Calamares are also cooked *en su tinta* (in their own ink) – black, shiny and very good – and as *fritos a la romana* (floured and fried squid rings).

stuffed calamares
calamares rellenos

5 tablespoons extra virgin olive oil

1 medium onion, finely chopped

16 ready prepared baby squid with tentacles, about 7 cm long (see note)

50 g chorizo, finely chopped

½ teaspoon chilli flakes

70 g pine nuts

2 garlic cloves, finely chopped

2 tablespoons chopped fresh flat leaf parsley, plus extra coarsely chopped, to serve

175 ml measured fresh breadcrumbs

Tomato sauce

2 tablespoons extra virgin olive oil

1 onion, finely chopped

1 garlic clove, finely chopped

½ teaspoon sugar

6 medium tomatoes, skinned, deseeded and finely chopped (retain any juices)

Serves 4

Heat 3 tablespoons of the oil in a frying pan, add the onion and fry until soft and pale golden. Add the chopped tentacles and fry until pale. Add the chorizo and fry until the fat runs out into the onion. Stir in the chile flakes.

Toast the pine nuts in a dry frying pan for a minute or so until golden. Take care, because they will burn easily. Transfer to a plate to cool.

Meanwhile, put the garlic, parsley, the breadcrumbs and half the pine nuts in a processor and pulse until fine. Add to the pan and let cool.

To make the tomato sauce, heat the oil in a flameproof casserole dish, add the onion and garlic and fry until pale gold. Increase the heat, add the sugar and the tomatoes with their juice, then simmer for a few minutes.

Stuff the squid with the cold mixture and close with a cocktail stick. Heat the remaining oil in a frying pan, add the stuffed squid and fry on both sides until pale golden, about 2 minutes on each side. Add to the casserole dish and cook in a preheated oven at 190°C (375°F) Gas 5 for 15 minutes. Remove from the oven, sprinkle with parsley and remaining toasted pine nuts and serve.

Note If you have to clean the squid yourself, first pull off the tentacles. Rinse out the bodies and discard the stiff transparent quill if any. Cut the tentacles away from the head, and discard the head. Chop the tentacles into small pieces.

Zarzuela is from the Catalan word for light opera or variety show – a medley in fact – and this medley is a feast in a pan. Add any fish or shellfish you like, as long as it's firm enough not to flake into shreds – use whatever is available on the day.

12 mussels, scrubbed and debearded

12 clams, scrubbed and rinsed

250 ml dry white wine

250 g monkfish fillet, skinned and cut into large chunks

250 g halibut fillet, cut into large chunks

6 large peeled prawns, tail fins on

5 tablespoons virgin olive oil

6 cooked langoustines or extra prawns

sea salt and freshly ground black pepper

2 lemons, cut into wedges, to serve

Picada

2 slices fried white bread, cut into cubes

2 garlic cloves, coarsely chopped

9 almonds, coarsely chopped

125 ml extra virgin olive oil

Sofregit

2 tablespoons olive oil

1 onion, finely chopped

1 garlic clove, crushed

2 teaspoons sweet paprika (pimentón dulce)

200 g canned chopped tomatoes

½ teaspoon saffron threads, soaked in 1 tablespoon boiling water

3 bay leaves

sea salt and freshly ground black pepper

Serves 4

zarzuela
zarzuela de mariscos

To make the picada, put the fried bread in a small processor with the garlic and almonds and blend finely. With the motor running, gradually add the oil to form a loose paste.

To prepare the mussels and clams, put the wine in a large saucepan and bring to the boil. Add the mussels and clams, cover and cook over medium heat for about 2 minutes – shake the pan after 1 minute – until all the shells have opened. Discard any that haven't. Pour into a colander set over a bowl to catch all the liquid. Transfer the mussels and clams to a bowl and cover loosely. Reserve the liquid to use in the sofregit.

To make the sofregit, heat the oil in a saucepan, add the onion and garlic and fry gently until pale golden and soft. Stir in the paprika, tomatoes and saffron and its soaking water. Pour the mussel liquid carefully through a fine-meshed sieve, leaving any sediment behind. Add the bay leaves, salt and pepper. Cover and cook over medium heat for 10 minutes. Add a little water if the mixture gets too thick.

Season the monkfish, halibut and prawns with salt and pepper. Heat 2 tablespoons of the oil in a frying pan, add the pieces of monkfish and halibut and fry until lightly golden on both sides. Remove to a plate and keep them warm. Deglaze the pan with 3 tablespoons water and pour into the simmering sofregit.

Wipe the frying pan, add the remaining 3 tablespoons oil and the prawns and fry just until they turn pink on both sides. Add the langoustines to heat through for 1 minute, turning frequently. Pour in the cooked sofregit and add the rest of the seafood, including the mussels and clams. Heat very gently for a few minutes to ensure everything is cooked through. Loosen the picada with a little liquid from the pan and fold into the seafood. Serve with the lemon wedges.

A mixture of very finely chopped vegetables forms the basis of this dish. In can be served either very hot straight from the oven or left until cold, which I like in summer. In winter, you could use fresh herrings instead. In true Spanish style, eat it with bread to mop up the juices – no Spaniard would ever sit down to a meal without lots of good bread.

baked sardines
sardinas en cazuela

5 tablespoons extra virgin olive oil

1 red pepper, deseeded and finely chopped

2 medium onions, finely chopped

3 garlic cloves, crushed

2 large tomatoes, skinned, deseeded and cut into 3 cm cubes

1 teaspoon hot paprika (pimentón picante)

a pinch of saffron

¼ teaspoon ground cumin

2 bay leaves

2 tablespoons chopped fresh flat leaf parsley, plus extra leaves to serve

9–12 fresh sardine fillets (depending on the size of the dish)

fine sea salt and freshly ground black pepper

a medium cazuela or ovenproof dish

Serves 4–6

Heat 3 tablespoons of the oil in a frying pan, add the red pepper, onions and garlic and cook gently until softened but not coloured, 8–10 minutes. Add the tomatoes, paprika, saffron, cumin and bay leaves and cook for a further 5–8 minutes (add a little water if the mixture sticks to the pan) until completely cooked. Season with salt and pepper and fold in the parsley.

Put the sardine fillets on a tray skin side down and sprinkle with a little salt and pepper.

Arrange one-third of the fillets skin side up in the cazuela or ovenproof dish, cover with one-third of the cooked mixture. Repeat twice more – when adding the last layer, let the silver sardine skin peek through. Grind over a little more pepper and spoon over the rest of the oil.

Bake the cazuela in a preheated oven at 190°C (375°F) Gas 5 for 15–20 minutes until sizzling. Sprinkle with parsley leaves, then serve.

Orense is on the river Miño in Galicia, a region of fabulous fish and passionate fish lovers. Although most of us have to be content with farmed fish, this area is famous for its trout-fishing streams. There is a Spanish saying that trout is never better than when *fresca, frita y fría* – in other words 'fresh, fried and cold'. This recipe is testament to this, except it is also wonderful served hot. Excellent with a white wine made from the local grape variety, Albariño – fruity yet delicate.

fresh fried trout
truchas fritas a la orensana

3 tablespoons olive oil

150 g cubed Spanish panceta, bacon lardons or ham

2 trout, cleaned

2 tablespoons plain flour, seasoned with salt and pepper

1 garlic clove, cut into slivers

2 tablespoons chopped fresh flat leaf parsley

sea salt and freshly ground black pepper

1 lemon, cut into wedges, to serve

Serves 2

Heat 1 tablespoon of the oil in a frying pan, add the panceta and fry until just golden. Remove to a plate.

Dust the fish with the seasoned flour. Open the bellies, season with salt and pepper and put in the garlic slivers.

Heat the remaining oil in the frying pan, add the trout and fry over medium heat for 3 minutes on each side. Increase the heat and cook for a further 2 minutes on each side. Transfer to hot plates, then return the panceta to the pan to warm through. Spoon the panceta on top of the trout and sprinkle with parsley and pepper. Serve hot with lemon wedges, or leave until cold.

Note *Panceta* is Spanish streaky bacon, like Italian pancetta. *Panceta ahumada* is smoked streaky bacon. Both are available cut from slabs in Spanish shops.

Sea bass has the perfect texture for this dish, which is my favourite fish recipe. Serve with lots of bread and enjoy a nice crisp wine made from the Parellada grape, perfect for a summer lunch under a vine-laden awning. I use virgin olive oil, not extra virgin: extra virgin is too powerful for the mildly acidic flavours of this dish.

sea bass in vinaigrette with capers and parsley
lubina en vinagreta con alcaparras

400 ml dry white wine

zest from 1 unwaxed lemon, peeled off in wide strips

zest from 1 unwaxed orange, peeled off in wide strips

3–4 large shallots or red onions, finely sliced

a handful of parsley stalks

1 kg sea bass fillets (4–8, depending on size)

2 tablespoons white wine vinegar

½ teaspoon caster sugar

6 tablespoons virgin olive oil

3 tablespoons capers, drained and rinsed

3 tablespoons fresh flat leaf parsley leaves

coarse sea salt and freshly ground black pepper

Serves 4

Working in 2 batches, put 200 ml of the wine and 250 ml cold water in a shallow pan such as a non-stick frying pan. Add half the strips of lemon and orange zest, 1 of the shallots, half the parsley stalks and salt. Add half the sea bass fillets and slowly bring to a gentle simmer, about 5 minutes. As soon as the liquid starts to bubble, take the pan off the heat and leave for 2 minutes. Transfer the fillets to a serving dish and keep them warm, while you repeat with the second batch, using 200 ml wine, 250 ml cold water, the remaining strips of zest, 1 shallot, the remaining parsley and some salt.

Meanwhile soak the remaining shallots in the vinegar for about 3 minutes. Drain off the vinegar into a bowl and use to make the dressing. Reserve the soaked shallots.

Add the sugar, salt and pepper to the vinegar and whisk in the olive oil, a little at a time. Mix in the shallots, capers and parsley and pour over the fish fillets while they are still hot. Let cool and eat after 1–2 hours.

Marmitako is from the Basque region and the name comes from the French word *marmite* – a tall, straight-sided stewpot made from copper, iron or earthenware. The fishermen used to make this stew on board their boats, using bonito or albacore tuna from the Bay of Biscay, and mopping up the soupy juices with lots of delicious fried bread. Try one of the crisp, grapey, thirst-quenching white wines from the Basque region, such as Chacoli de Getaria and Chacoli de Bizkaia.

tuna and potato stew
marmitako

1 small red pepper

1 small yellow pepper

1 small green pepper

3 tablespoons extra virgin olive oil

1 large onion, finely chopped

2 garlic cloves, finely chopped

5 tomatoes, skinned, deseeded and chopped (reserve any juices)

½ teaspoon sweet paprika (pimentón dulce)

1 bay leaf

500 g potatoes, peeled and cut into 1 cm slices

2 slices of fresh tuna, 500 g each, cut into 6 chunky pieces each

2 tablespoons parsley leaves, torn

coarse sea salt and freshly ground black pepper

Fried bread

6 slices of white bread, cut into triangles

extra virgin olive oil, for frying

Serves 4–6

Halve and deseed the red, yellow and green peppers and cut the flesh into 1 cm cubes.

Heat the oil in a heatproof casserole, add the onion, garlic and peppers and fry over low heat until softened but not coloured, 12–15 minutes. Increase the heat and stir in the tomatoes and their juice. When the mixture starts to thicken, add the paprika, bay leaf, salt and pepper.

Stir in the potatoes and 400 ml boiling water and simmer gently for about 15 minutes until the potatoes are cooked.

Meanwhile, to make the fried bread, heat the olive oil in a large frying pan, add the triangles of bread and fry on both sides until golden. Remove and drain on kitchen paper.

Season the pieces of tuna 10 minutes before cooking. Add the tuna to the casserole and after about 30 seconds, when the underside turns pale, turn the pieces over and turn off the heat. Leave for 5 minutes. Sprinkle with parsley and serve with the triangles of fried bread.

Spaniards insist on the freshest of fish. Even in Madrid, in the middle of Spain, the catch is rushed from every coast to reach markets and restaurants in superb condition. This recipe is a good dish for a large family. If red bream isn't available, use gilt-head bream (dorada) or red snapper.

baked red bream
besugo al horno

800 g red bream fillets, cut into 6 cm pieces

½ lemon, cut into thin wedges

3 tablespoons fine fresh breadcrumbs

2 garlic cloves, crushed

2 tablespoons hot paprika (pimentón picante)

1 tablespoon finely chopped flat leaf parsley

4 medium potatoes, thinly sliced

125 ml extra virgin olive oil

12 black olives

sea salt and freshly ground black pepper

an oiled ovenproof dish large enough to hold the fish in a single layer

Serves 4

Make a slash on the skin of each piece of fish, lightly salt them all over, then insert a lemon wedge into each slash.

Mix the breadcrumbs, garlic, paprika and parsley in a bowl.

Put a layer of the potatoes in the oiled ovenproof dish. Sprinkle the potatoes with salt and pepper and spoon over 2 tablespoons of oil and 4 tablespoons water. Bake in a preheated oven at 190°C (375°F) Gas 5 for 30–40 minutes.

Put the fish on top, sprinkle with the breadcrumb mixture and pour the remaining olive oil over the top. Pour 2 more tablespoons of water around the sides of the dish (so the crumbs don't get wet) and bake for a further 10 minutes.

Dot with the olives, cover the dish and cook for a further 5–10 minutes until the potatoes are soft and the fish flakes easily.

The traditional cooking pan for this dish is the cazuela – a wide, flat, terracotta casserole, glazed except for the base. It has amazing heat-retaining properties and is excellent for dishes that rely on slow, even heat. If cooking on top of the stove, use a heat-diffusing mat. To season a cazuela, see page 23.

hake in garlic sauce with clams
merluza al pil pil con almejas

500 g clams

90 ml dry white wine

6 hake or cod steaks, cut 2 cm thick through the bone

150 ml olive oil

4 garlic cloves, thinly slivered

4 tablespoons chopped fresh flat leaf parsley

sea salt and freshly ground black pepper

a cazuela or heavy frying pan

Serves 4–6

Put the clams and wine in a saucepan over high heat. As they open, remove them to a bowl and cover with clingfilm. Discard any that fail to open. Strain the cooking juices through a muslin-lined sieve and set aside.

Put the fish on a plate and sprinkle with salt 10 minutes before cooking.

Put the oil and garlic in a cazuela or heavy frying pan and heat gently so the garlic turns golden slowly and doesn't burn. Remove the garlic with a slotted spoon and keep until ready to serve.

Pour about two-thirds of the oil into a jug and add the fish to the oil left in the pan. Cook over very low heat, moving the pan in a circular motion – keep taking it off the heat so it doesn't cook too quickly (the idea is to encourage the oozing of the juices instead of letting them fry and burn). Add the remaining oil little by little as you move the pan, so an emulsion starts to form. When all the oil has been added, remove the fish to a plate and keep it warm. Put the pan back on the heat, add the reserved clam juices and stir to form a creamy sauce.

Return the fish to the pan, add the chopped parsley and continue to cook until the fish is done, about 5 minutes. Just before serving, add the clams and heat through. Serve sprinkled with the fried garlic.

meat and poultry
carnes

I like this dish served on bread fried in good olive oil – a bit rich, but very delicious. Try to find a smoked salted bacon from Galicia called *panceta ahumada*; otherwise use smoked bacon lardons. Smoked paprika is easy to find now, but unsmoked will be good too. In cooking, I use manzanilla, a dry sherry named after the camomile herb; it has a slightly bitter, astringent note like its namesake.

sautéed chicken livers
hígadillos salteados

3 tablespoons extra virgin olive oil

1 medium onion, finely chopped

2 garlic cloves, crushed

125 g chopped smoked Spanish panceta
or smoked bacon lardons

4 sprigs of thyme

250 g chicken livers, trimmed and cut in half

¼ teaspoon smoked hot paprika
(pimentón picante), plus extra for dusting

3 tablespoons manzanilla sherry

2 tablespoons chopped fresh flat leaf parsley

sea salt and freshly ground black pepper

Fried bread

6 slices of white bread, crusts removed,
cut into triangles

extra virgin olive oil, for frying

Serves 4

To make the fried bread, heat the olive oil in a large frying pan, add the triangles of bread and fry on both sides until golden. Remove and drain on kitchen paper.

Heat 2 tablespoons of the olive oil in a frying pan, add the onion and garlic and fry over low heat for 5 minutes until completely softened but not coloured.

Increase the heat, add the panceta and thyme and fry for about 5 minutes until everything is golden. Transfer to a plate.

Wipe the pan with kitchen paper. Heat the remaining oil in the pan, then add the chicken livers, paprika, salt and pepper and fry over high heat until golden on both sides and soft in the middle (they will spit, so take care).

Transfer to the plate with the onion mixture. Deglaze the pan with the manzanilla until almost evaporated, then return the contents of the plate to the pan. Add the parsley, stir and serve immediately on the fried bread. Dust with a little extra paprika.

Huge quantities of garlic are essential for this recipe and should be eaten squashed onto the chicken. My sister-in-law, a long-time Spanish resident, is addicted to it, judging by all the finger-licking and moans of approval, all spoken in her best Spanish. I have not quite mastered the accent, but I have managed to impress her with my recipe. Pollo al Ajillo is served as a tapa or as a main dish. It is eaten with the fingers, and in restaurants is usually served with fries (page 99), so it is certainly a hands-on dish (lots of paper napkins will be required). A modern Penedès white wine made from unoaked Chardonnay would be a suitable companion.

chicken with garlic
pollo al ajillo

1 tablespoon sweet paprika (pimentón dulce)

1 tablespoon plain flour

1.75 kg chicken pieces, such as thighs and breasts (but no drumsticks)

100 ml virgin olive oil

15 garlic cloves, unpeeled but bruised slightly

1 fresh bay leaf

125 ml medium dry sherry

1 tablespoon coarsely chopped fresh flat leaf parsley

sea salt and freshly ground black pepper

a heat-diffusing mat

Serves 4

Put the paprika, flour, salt and pepper in a plastic bag and shake to mix. Add the chicken pieces and toss again until the chicken is evenly coated. Leave in the bag for 30 minutes or longer.

Heat the oil in a frying pan, add the garlic and fry for 2 minutes, then remove with a slotted spoon. Add the chicken pieces (if necessary do half at a time, but remember to remove half the garlic-infused oil) and fry for 5 minutes. Add the garlic and continue frying for 5 minutes until the chicken is golden on all sides.

Add the bay leaf and sherry and bring to the boil. Lower the heat and simmer gently on a heat-diffusing mat for about 30 minutes until tender. (Breast pieces will cook faster, so remove them about 10 minutes before the end of cooking.) Pile onto a serving platter and sprinkle with parsley.

Note Although Pollo al Ajillo is traditionally cooked on top of the stove, it could be baked in a preheated oven at 190°C (375°F) Gas 5 for 35 minutes or until cooked through.

Seville, on the river Guadalquivir in Andalucía, is the source of this recipe. Duck are plentiful on the tidal marshlands, Las Marismas, while endless groves of olives produce both fruit and oil. Olives were introduced to Spain around the 5th century BC by the Carthaginians and the Greeks. There are many varieties to choose; look for aragón (dark with a hint of pink), the small, black cacereña, the small, green, rather astringent manzanilla (yes, manzanilla is an olive too) and greenish–purple arbequina, with its spicy flavour.

duck with olives
pato con aceitunas

4 duck breasts, the fat scored into diamonds

4 sprigs of thyme

2 tablespoons manzanilla sherry

3 tablespoons olive oil

10 shallots, separated into lobes

2 medium onions, finely chopped

3 garlic cloves, crushed

4 tablespoons dry white wine

20 black and 20 green olives, flesh sliced off the stones in 4 long pieces

sea salt and freshly ground black pepper

Serves 4

Put the duck in a shallow dish, sprinkle with the thyme, sherry, salt and pepper and let marinate for about 30 minutes.

Pat the duck dry with kitchen paper and heat a frying pan on a high heat until smoking. Add the duck skin side down and fry without oil on one side only for 5 minutes until deep golden brown. Remove the duck to a plate. Drain off the duck fat and keep to cook potatoes on another occasion. Wipe the pan, heat 1 tablespoon of the oil, add the shallots and fry until pale golden. Transfer to the plate with the duck.

Heat the remaining oil, add the onions and garlic and fry gently for 5 minutes until softened but not coloured. Increase the heat, add the wine and bring to the boil. Transfer to a shallow ovenproof casserole, add the shallots and duck breasts, skin side up, and the marinade. Cook in a preheated oven at 220°C (425°F) Gas 7 for 5–8 minutes. If you prefer the duck to be more well done, cook for 3–5 minutes longer.

Add the olives and cook for a further 5 minutes. Slice the duck breasts lengthways, then serve with the olive and onion mixture.

Note The Guadalquivir is the northern boundary of the sherry region, so with a dish like this, you might choose an aged fino; still pale straw-coloured, but with more intensity and depth than a young fino. Also suitable would be a lighter, modern Rioja, or another lighter style such as Pinot Noir (little grown in Spain).

2 tablespoons plain flour, seasoned with salt and pepper

1 kg rabbit pieces

the liver from the rabbit, or 1 tablespoon coarsely chopped almonds

5 tablespoons olive oil

150 g cubed smoked Spanish panceta or smoked bacon lardons

1 large onion

4 tomatoes, skinned, deseeded and chopped (reserve the juices)

100 ml red wine

2 sprigs of rosemary

1 teaspoon fennel seeds, coarsely crushed to release their flavour

500 g new potatoes

a large pinch of saffron

1 dried chilli, such as the Spanish ñora, deseeded and coarsely chopped

2 garlic cloves, coarsely chopped

25 g dark chocolate, chopped

3 tablespoons coarsely chopped fresh flat leaf parsley

sea salt and freshly ground black pepper

a heatproof casserole or cazuela, 20–25 cm diameter

a heat-diffusing mat

kitchen foil

Serves 4

Though hot chocolate is one of Spain's favourite drinks, chocolate is also used in braised dishes. It was brought to Spain from Nicaragua in the early 16th century in the form of beans, but at first no one knew what to do with them. For years, Spain guarded it jealously and its export to other parts of Europe was prohibited. Eventually, the prohibition failed and it became everyone's favourite vice. This rabbit dish, by the way, doesn't contain tarragon – it is from the Catalan city of Tarragona, south of Barcelona. A good wine companion would be a red from the Priorat DOC.

braised rabbit
conejo a la tarragona

Put the seasoned flour in a plastic bag, add the rabbit pieces and toss to coat. (If not using liver, use the chopped almonds at the end of the recipe to help thicken the sauce.)

Heat 3 tablespoons of the oil in a frying pan, add the rabbit and liver and fry until slightly golden on both sides. Transfer to a bowl, leaving the oil behind. Add the panceta and fry until golden, then transfer to the bowl with the rabbit.

Heat the remaining oil in a heatproof casserole or cazuela, add the onion and fry gently for about 10 minutes until softened but not browned. Add the tomatoes and cook over medium heat for 4 minutes. Add the wine, increase the heat and boil for 2 minutes. Add the rosemary, fennel seeds, salt, pepper and the rabbit, but not the liver. Cover with a lid or foil, transfer to a preheated oven at 180°C (350°F) Gas 4 and cook for 30 minutes.

Meanwhile, parboil the potatoes in a saucepan of salted water. Put the saffron, chilli, garlic and chocolate in a small blender. Chop the liver, if using, and add to the blender. Add 50 ml hot water and blend to a smooth paste. If using chopped almonds instead of the liver, add them at this point. Add the paste and the potatoes to the rabbit and cook for about 30 minutes more until everything is tender. Sprinkle with parsley and serve.

In Madrid, this very basic dish would appear with fried potatoes and a simple tomato sauce. However, I was introduced to it served with a sauce from the Valencia and Alicante region – Salsa Salmoretta, which is also the classic accompaniment for the fish and rice dish, Arroz Abanda (page 10). Serve it with a dry red such as a modern Rioja, a blend of Tempranillo and Cabernet Sauvignon.

lamb cutlets
chulitas de cordero

3 garlic cloves, crushed

2 teaspoons sweet paprika (pimentón dulce)

4 sprigs of thyme (leaves picked off 2 of them)

3 tablespoons olive oil

12 lamb cutlets, trimmed

sea salt and freshly ground black pepper

Salsa salmoretta

1 large shallot, finely sliced

3 ripe medium tomatoes

2 garlic cloves, finely chopped

1 dried hot red chilli, such as guindilla, deseeded and finely chopped

1 tablespoon finely chopped fresh flat leaf parsley

90 ml olive oil

1½ teaspoons red wine vinegar

sea salt and freshly ground black pepper

Serves 4

To marinate the cutlets, put the garlic, paprika, thyme sprigs and leaves, olive oil, salt and pepper in a flat dish and stir to mix. Add the cutlets, turn to coat and let marinate for 2 hours or overnight.

Heat a ridged stove-top grill pan until smoking, then add the cutlets and cook for 3 minutes on each side. Alternatively, cook on a preheated barbecue.

Meanwhile, to make the salsa salmoretta, put the shallot in a bowl and cover with cold water.

Cut a cross in the top of each tomato and put under a preheated hot grill for 5 minutes, turning twice, until the skins are wrinkled and the flesh is soft. Peel, deseed and finely chop the flesh, then put in a bowl.

Meanwhile, crush the garlic, chilli and parsley to a paste with a mortar and pestle. Work in two-thirds of the chopped tomatoes. Drain the shallot and crush half of it with the tomatoes. Still stirring with the pestle, gradually add the oil to emulsify. Stir in the vinegar, the remaining tomatoes and shallot, salt and pepper.

Serve the salsa with the cutlets.

Variation Substitute pork chops to make Chulitas de Cerdo. Both lamb and pork *chulitas* are delicious cooked on the barbecue.

The best-known dish from the region of Aragón, this is coloured and flavoured with choricero, a fat dried pepper about 8 cm long. It is mild, yet sweet and rich, and also provides the colour and flavour in chorizo sausages. The sauce should be quite dry – not liquid like a stew. Cook it slowly to reduce and coat the meat.

Chicken or veal is also good cooked this way. Spanish veal is pink, not pale, because the calves aren't intensively reared. As a wine match, try a Somontano DO from the Pyrenees, based on Cabernet Sauvignon, or another soft red from Aragón, made from Garnacha (Grenache).

braised lamb with peppers and tomatoes
cordero a la chilindrón

4 tablespoons olive oil

1 large onion, finely chopped

4 garlic cloves, crushed

1 dried choricero or other mild red chilli, soaked in boiling water for 20 minutes

1.5 kg leg of lamb, meat removed from the bone and cut into 2.5 cm pieces

1 jar of Spanish roasted peppers, 285 g, drained and coarsely chopped

400 g canned chopped tomatoes

leaves from a small bunch of flat leaf parsley

coarse sea salt and freshly ground black pepper

a heat-diffusing mat

Serves 4

Heat 2 tablespoons of the oil in a heatproof casserole, add the onion and garlic and fry for about 7 minutes until soft and just golden. Scrape the flesh from the soaked chilli and mix it into the onions. Transfer to a plate and wipe out the casserole.

Heat the remaining oil in the casserole and fry the lamb in batches until golden on all sides. Fold in the onion mixture, the peppers, tomatoes, salt and pepper. Bring to the boil and immediately reduce the heat so the surface just gently bubbles. Cook uncovered for 30 minutes, stirring occasionally to prevent it sticking (use a heat-diffusing mat for best results). If it looks so thick that it prevents the meat from cooking, stir in a little boiling water to loosen the mixture.

Cover and continue cooking for a further 30 minutes until the meat is very tender. Remove from the heat and let rest for about 5 minutes. Serve sprinkled with the parsley leaves.

Variation Cook uncovered in a preheated oven at 180°C (350°F) Gas 4 for 30 minutes, then cover and cook for a further 30 minutes.

Note If you prefer, instead of dried chilli, use 1 teaspoon hot paprika (pimentón picante) and 2 teaspoons sweet paprika (pimentón dulce).

Ask your butcher to prepare the pork loin ready for stuffing.
To prepare it yourself, see the note below. Serve with a
light, juicy red from Rioja.

stuffed pork loin
lomo de cerdo relleno

about 75 g blanched almonds

3 tablespoons olive oil

1 medium onion, chopped

1 garlic clove, crushed

50 g cubed Spanish panceta,
pancetta cubetti or bacon lardons

200 g salchicha sausages or any good spicy
fresh pork sausage, skins removed

1½ tablespoons finely chopped
fresh flat leaf parsley

1 kg loin of pork, without rind

200 ml dry white wine

coarse sea salt and freshly
ground black pepper

Serves 4–6

Put the almonds in a dry frying pan and cook over gentle heat, shaking the
pan, until lightly golden. Take care, because they burn easily. Tip onto a
plate, let cool, then chop finely.

Heat 2 tablespoons of the oil in a frying pan, add the onion and garlic and
fry for about 5 minutes until softened but not coloured. Transfer to a plate
and let cool. Wipe out the pan, add the panceta, fry without oil until
golden, then add to the onions.

When the onion mixture is cool, put it in a bowl with the sausage meat,
toasted almonds and parsley, season with salt and pepper and mix well.

Open out the pork, sprinkle with salt and pepper, cover and set aside for
30 minutes.

Spread the stuffing all over the inside surface of the pork, leaving a 2 cm
border all around. Roll up and tie with kitchen string at 2 cm intervals.
Season the outside with salt and pepper.

Heat the remaining oil in a heatproof casserole, add the pork and fry on
all sides until golden. Add the wine and bring to the boil. Transfer the
casserole to a preheated oven at 230°C (450°F) Gas 8 and cook
uncovered for 20 minutes. Reduce the heat to 180°C (350°F) Gas 4, cover
the casserole and cook for another 20 minutes for each 500 g in weight.
Uncover for the last 10 minutes. Let the meat rest for 10–15 minutes, then
slice thickly and serve.

Note To prepare the loin ready for stuffing, put the pork loin, flesh side
down, on a cutting board – the loin should be at right angles to yourself.
Using a long knife, make an incision about 2 cm deep the length of the
loin. Roll back the edge and continue cutting lengthways keeping a
2 cm thickness. Follow the line of the circle, folding back the meat so it
lies flat on the board. You will have a flat piece of meat, ready to spread
with the stuffing.

A robust country dish from Asturias in the cooler north of Spain, fabada consists of typical local ingredients; *fabes* (fat white beans), *lacón* (cured pork), panceta (cured streaky bacon), morcilla (black pudding) and chorizo, all cooked in the same pot. It was typical winter peasant fare and has become a classic dish, appreciated all over the country. Serve it with cornbread and cider, specialities of Asturias, or with a classic Rioja.

beans with ham
fabada asturiana

350 g fabes (large dried white beans), cannellini or white haricot beans, covered with cold water and soaked overnight

2 bay leaves

a large pinch of saffron threads, toasted in a dry frying pan and ground to a powder

1 onion, cut into quarters through the root

350 g piece of cured pork shoulder or lacón (Spanish cured pork), soaked overnight if salty

150 g morcilla or other black pudding (optional)

150 g sweet chorizo, or other chorizo suitable for cooking

1 tablespoon extra virgin olive oil

2 garlic cloves, crushed

1 tablespoon sweet paprika (pimentón dulce)

a heat-diffusing mat

Serves 4–6

Drain the beans and put in a saucepan with 1.5 litres cold water and the bay leaves. Bring to the boil for 5 minutes, then throw in 250 ml cold water to *asustar* or 'scare' the beans. Immediately skim any froth off the surface and boil again for 5 minutes. Repeat the scare treatment and skim again.

Return to the boil for 5 minutes, add the saffron and onion, lower the heat to a simmer and add the pork, morcilla, if using, and chorizo. Simmer very gently using a heat-diffusing mat for about 2 hours until everything has cooked. Alternatively, bring to the boil on top of the stove, then cook in a preheated oven at 180°C (350°F) Gas 4 for the same time.

During this time, keep the water level topped up to cover everything and occasionally skim and discard the red oil that rises to the surface.

When everything is soft, remove the meats, put in a deep serving dish and keep them warm. Put the beans in a bowl and keep them warm too.

Using a baster, remove 250 ml liquid from the pot, leaving any red oil behind. Heat the olive oil in a frying pan, add the garlic and paprika and fry until crisp. Add the 250 ml liquid to deglaze the pan and pour into a blender with 3 tablespoons of cooked beans and the onion. Pulse to form a coarse purée, then stir into the bowl of beans.

Cut the meat into thick slices and return to the serving dish. Add the bean mixture and serve.

Spanish fries and pimientos de Padrón are the classic accompaniments for grilled meats. Spanish fries, served with almost every restaurant main course in Spain, are the best I've ever tasted, and the secret is the good olive oil used for frying. Good companions would be a hearty Tempranillo or Garnacha-based red from Rioja or a rustic red from La Mancha such as Marqués de Griñon.

4 entrecôte steaks, 2 cm thick

3 garlic cloves, crushed

3 tablespoons finely chopped flat leaf parsley

5 tablespoons extra virgin olive oil

freshly squeezed juice of 1 lemon

coarse sea salt and freshly ground black pepper

Salsa de aceitunas

4 tablespoons olive oil

1 tablespoon sherry vinegar

125 g mixed pitted green and black olives

2 garlic cloves, crushed

2 firm tomatoes, skinned, deseeded and finely chopped

sea salt and freshly ground black pepper

To serve (optional)

pimientos de Padrón (page 16)

Spanish fries (see note)

Serves 4

pan-grilled steaks with olive sauce
entrecôte a la plancha con salsa de aceitunas

Put the steaks in a flat dish, sprinkle with the garlic, pepper and half the parsley, pour over the oil and lemon juice and rub in. Set aside for 2 hours or overnight in the refrigerator. Remove from the refrigerator 30 minutes before cooking, and sprinkle with salt.

Meanwhile, to make the salsa, put the oil in a bowl and whisk in the sherry vinegar. Put the olives in a processor and pulse to chop into small, evenly sized bits (not a purée). Put in the bowl with the oil mixture, add the garlic and tomatoes and season lightly with salt and pepper.

When ready to cook the steak, heat a ridged stove-top grill pan over high heat. When smoking, add the steaks and cook for 1½ minutes on each side for rare, 2 for medium and 2½–3 for well done. Alternatively, cook on the barbecue. Sprinkle with the rest of the parsley and serve with the salsa together with the pimientos de Padrón and Spanish fries, if using.

Note To make Spanish fries, put 750 g potatoes, such as Belle de Fontenay, into 6 mm slices, then into 6 mm fingers. Rinse well in cold water to remove the starch, then pat dry on kitchen paper.

Fill a deep-fryer with pure olive oil to the manufacturer's recommended level and heat to 180°C (350°F). Working in batches, fry the potatoes until golden, then drain on kitchen paper and keep hot.

JUDIAS DORADAS KILO 4.50€

JUDIAS CARITAS kilo 3.40€

JUDIAS MANTECA KILO 3.31.

HIGOS KILO 4.20€

PIÑONES 100GRAMOS 3.00€

PASAS -SIN HUESOS.- KILO 6.00€

UN-MANOJO 125 €

PIMIENTOS 0.49 EL 1/4

TOMATES Kilo

UN-MANOJO 1€

vegetables and pulses
verduras y legumbres secas

Asparagus served with *salsa mayonesa* (fresh mayo), *sel marina* (coarse sea salt) and *choricitos fritos* (sautéed sliced baby chorizos) is a simple dish. True wild asparagus grows on the edges of wheatfields in spring and is called *triguerros* after *trigo,* the Spanish word for 'wheat'. Sweet in flavour, it is a much paler green than our thin asparagus.

grilled wild asparagus
esparragos trigueros a la plancha

750 g thin asparagus
3 tablespoons olive oil
a pinch of fine sea salt
freshly ground black pepper

Mayonesa
1 garlic clove, finely chopped
2 teaspoons freshly squeezed lemon juice
a pinch of salt
1 egg yolk
150 ml olive oil

To serve
coarse sea salt
2 baby chorizos (choricitos), sliced,
then fried without oil in a dry frying pan

Serves 4

To make the mayonesa, put the garlic, half the lemon juice, a pinch of salt and a few drops of water in a mortar and pound to a paste. Add the egg yolk, grinding with the pestle in one direction. Gradually mix in the oil in drops. After adding 100 ml, add a little more of the lemon juice and continue slowly mixing in the oil until a thick emulsion forms. Taste and adjust the flavour with more salt and the remaining lemon juice if needed. Alternatively, use a blender or small food processor, but you will have to double the ingredients or the mixture won't cover the blades. Cover any leftovers with clingfilm, chill and keep for another use.

Trim the asparagus and peel away the papery triangular bits from the stalk. Put the oil, salt and pepper in a shallow dish, add the asparagus and turn to coat.

Heat a ridged stove-top grill pan until smoking. Add the asparagus, a batch at a time, turning the spears over when grill marks appear. They will take 1½–2½ minutes on each side. Serve while still hot with the mayonesa, sea salt and chorizos in small bowls.

Notes
• Spaniards claim to have invented mayonnaise (*mahonesa* or *mayonesa*), because it hails from Mahón in Menorca.
• White Rioja wine would have been a suitable companion for this dish, but Albariño has now overtaken it as Spain's most popular white wine variety.

My sister-in-law lived in Spain for many years and this is her favourite dish – so it must be good! It's also known as Acelgas a la Malageña, meaning Malaga-style, probably because raisins are grown in Malaga. Raisins and pine nuts in a dish show a Moorish influence. The smaller the leaves of chard, the more tender they will be.

swiss chard with raisins and pine nuts
acelgas con pasas y piñones

4 tablespoons pine nuts

4 tablespoons extra virgin olive oil

500 g Swiss chard (silver beet)

3 garlic cloves, thinly sliced, then chopped

100 g jamón serrano, chopped

3 tablespoons raisins, soaked and drained

coarse sea salt and freshly ground black pepper

Serves 4

Put the pine nuts and 1 tablespoon of the oil in a frying pan and fry over medium heat until golden. Take care because they burn easily. Transfer to a plate lined with kitchen paper and let cool.

Cut the chard and stalks into 2 cm pieces.

Heat the remaining oil in a frying pan, add the garlic and fry until just turning golden. Add the chard and ham and stir-fry until the chard wilts. Add the raisins and pine nuts and season lightly with pepper and salt (because the jamón serrano will already have added a salty flavour), then serve.

Note In Spain, vegetables are often served by themselves as a first course (often enormous) or as tapas, though the recipes in this chapter may be served as accompaniments to main courses in a very un-Spanish way. I like this Swiss chard recipe with trout, for instance. The market stalls groan with quantities of top-quality produce – and of course Spain is one of the most important producers of fruit and vegetables for the whole of Europe.

For this recipe, you need the tiny, often purplish-green variety of artichoke, available in early summer before it develops the hairy choke above the heart. Jamón serrano or country ham is delicious and can be eaten as it is or cooked as in this recipe.

If you serve this dish as part of a tapas selection, try it with a crisp sherry with a tangy sea-fresh quality, such as a manzanilla from the seaside town of Sanlúcar de Barrameda.

artichokes with cured ham
alcachofas con jamón serrano

1 lemon, halved

750 g very small artichokes

4 tablespoons extra virgin olive oil

8 slices jamón serrano, chopped

3 tablespoons chopped fresh flat leaf parsley

coarse sea salt and freshly ground black pepper

Serves 4

Fill a saucepan with water and squeeze in the lemon juice. Add the squeezed halves of lemon and some salt.

Trim the stalk of each artichoke to 1 cm, then trim off all the outer leaves until you reach the tender inner leaves. Cut the artichoke in half lengthways. As you prepare them, add to the pan of lemon water to stop them turning brown.

Bring to the boil, then lower the heat and simmer for about 7 minutes until just tender. Drain and dry.

Heat the oil in a frying pan, add the artichokes cut side down and fry for 5 minutes. Turn them over and fry the other side for a further 2 minutes. Add the jamón serrano and fry for a further 4 minutes until crisp and golden. Sprinkle with parsley and pepper and serve.

Note Spanish ham is of excellent quality. Jamón serrano is a delicious mountain ham, but the queen of hams is pata negra, from the handsome black Iberico pig. Pata negra is highly prized and expensive, so is used as a tapa in its own right, not for cooking.

Green beans are a great favourite in Spain. There are many recipes, but this is the one I like. If you add the dressing while the beans are still warm, they absorb more of the flavours. Delicious! I like this bean dish as a starter with a glass of fino sherry, as well as an accompaniment to meat or fish.

green beans with dressing
judias verdes a la vinagreta

1 pink banana shallot or 2 large shallots

2 tablespoons white wine vinegar

1 garlic clove

a pinch of sugar

4 tablespoons extra virgin olive oil

400 g thin green beans

1 hard-boiled egg, finely chopped

1 tablespoon chopped fresh flat leaf parsley

sea salt and freshly ground black pepper

Serves 6–8

Put the chopped shallot in a small bowl and pour over 1 tablespoon of the vinegar and 1 tablespoon water.

Crush the garlic to a paste with the sugar and a pinch of salt. Add pepper and the remaining vinegar and gradually whisk in the oil to make a dressing.

Cook the beans in a saucepan of boiling salted water for about 4 minutes until just cooked but still crisp. Drain, transfer to a serving dish, pour over the dressing and mix well. Rinse and drain the shallot. Sprinkle the shallot, egg and parsley on top of the beans and serve warm or cold.

Variations
• Serve sprinkled with Migas (page 19) instead of hard-boiled egg.
• Instead of hard-boiled egg, add a fried egg to make a delicious light dish for lunch.
• Instead of beans, use thick white asparagus or regular green asparagus.
• Add canned red kidney beans or chickpeas, drained and rinsed well, then mixed through the green beans.

Note For a more contemporary approach to sherry drinking, serve fino well-chilled in normal wine glasses. At 15 per cent alcohol, it is not very much stronger than a California Chardonnay, but drier and more tangy.

Every January, a uniquely Catalan festival, La Calçotada, celebrates the arrival of the *calçot* (pronounced 'cal-shot') and spring. These large spring onions are grilled over fires of vine cuttings until blackened and charred – eating them is a messy business and a real community affair. They are served wrapped in newspaper: this helps to complete the cooking and also steams off the charred outer layer so you can get to the sweet white flesh inside. This is a wonderful starter for a barbecue party – serve it with a bowl of the classic Salsa Romesco for dipping.

40 large spring onions or salad onions, with large bulbous white sections

2 tablespoons olive oil

coarse sea salt

Salsa romesco

20 blanched almonds, toasted in a dry frying pan

4 garlic cloves, unpeeled and blanched in cold water until soft, then peeled and chopped

2 dried chillies such as romesco or ñora, soaked in boiling water for 20 minutes, then deseeded and chopped, or 2 roasted red peppers from a jar

3 tomatoes, skinned, deseeded and chopped

2 teaspoons sweet paprika (pimentón dulce)

½ teaspoon chilli flakes

125 ml red wine vinegar

250 ml olive oil

sea salt and finely ground black pepper

Serves 4

grilled spring onion shoots with romesco sauce
calçots con salsa romesco

To make the salsa romesco, grind the almonds very finely in a clean coffee grinder. Put the ground almonds, garlic, chillies, tomatoes, paprika, chilli flakes and vinegar in a blender or food processor, then purée until smooth. Add salt and pepper, then drizzle in the oil gradually, with the motor running. Transfer to a small bowl.

Preheat a ridged stove-top grill pan or barbecue. Toss the spring onions in olive oil and salt, then grill until blackened and charred on the outside. Remove from the pan, then wrap in newspaper for 25 minutes until softened further. Serve with the salsa romesco and finger bowls, napkins and the traditional bibs if you want.

Note Fatter, more bulbous spring onions are often sold in supermarkets as 'salad onions'. Middle Eastern shops also stock very large varieties. Failing that, buy the largest spring onions you can find and decrease the cooking time.

If you don't have a coffee grinder, use ground almonds instead, although the sauce will lack a certain toasty flavour.

A clever Spanish housewife's trick for cooking dried beans is to *asustar* or 'scare' the beans with cold water several times during cooking. This will stop the beans softening too quickly on the outside before they cook on the inside. It's also said to stop the beans splitting, but to achieve this, they must always be covered with liquid. I find it's also an effective way of quickly stopping them from boiling over – and also helps when you skim the froth so you don't remove the solids too. This recipe is found in the fishing villages of Asturias and Cantabria on the Bay of Biscay; for me it's comfort food, fit for kings.

white beans with clams
alubias blancas con almejas

250 g alubias (Spanish dried white beans), or dried white haricot or cannellini beans, soaked for 24 hours or overnight

1 onion, halved

3 garlic cloves, peeled

1 carrot, halved

1 fresh bay leaf

a sprig of parsley

a small pinch of saffron, soaked in 1 tablespoon boiling water

salt

crusty bread, to serve

Clams

125 ml dry white wine

36 small clams

4 tablespoons olive oil

1 onion, finely chopped

2 garlic cloves, crushed

1 tablespoon sweet paprika (pimentón dulce)

1 medium dried red chilli, such as guindilla or chipotle, deseeded and roughly ground

2 tablespoons coarsely chopped fresh flat leaf parsley

coarse sea salt and freshly ground black pepper

a medium-size piece of muslin

Serves 4

Drain the soaked beans and put in a large saucepan with 800 ml cold water.

Add the onion halves, garlic, carrot, bay leaf and parsley and bring slowly to the boil. When the froth threatens to boil over, splash 200 ml cold water into the pan to 'scare' the beans. Skim off the froth, return to the boil and simmer for 10 minutes. Splash another 200 ml cold water into the pan, return to simmering point, then continue cooking for about 1 hour until tender. Remove the onion, carrot and parsley, add salt and cook for another 5 minutes. Drain over a bowl, then put the beans back in the pan with the saffron, its soaking water and 100 ml of the bean cooking liquid. Keep the lid on until ready to use. This stage can be done in advance.

To prepare the clams, heat the wine in a saucepan until boiling, add a little salt, then add the clams. Cook, covered, for about 2 minutes until they open (discard any that don't). Drain through a colander set over a bowl and cover the colander with a plate. Rinse out the saucepan, add the oil and heat for 30 seconds. Add the onion and garlic, cover and cook over low heat for about 10 minutes without browning. Stir in the paprika and a little salt and pepper.

Remove half the clams from their shells and discard the shells. Add all the clams to the onion mixture and carefully pour the clam liquid through a muslin-lined sieve into the pan, taking care to leave 1 cm in the bottom of the bowl because this may contain some grit. Heat the mixture just enough to warm up the clams.

Heat the beans and add the clam mixture. Ladle into heated soup plates. Sprinkle with parsley and serve with bread.

I use small brown lentils because they stay firm during cooking, but the big green ones called castellanas have a good flavour too. Lentil hotpots are the hearty comfort food of the Pyrenean valleys of Aragón. They are sometimes cooked with a ham bone for flavour, then served with delicious Spanish morcilla (black pudding) and vegetables.

Suitable companions for this dish would be elegant reds made from blends of Cabernet Sauvignon and the local Tempranillo, such as Somontano, softer reds based on Garnacha or easy-drinking Campode Borja.

250 g small lentils, rinsed

3 tablespoons extra virgin olive oil

1 onion, finely chopped

1 garlic clove, crushed

25 g butter

100 g small chestnut mushrooms

100 g oyster mushrooms, cut in half if large

3 tablespoons chopped fresh flat leaf parsley

1 teaspoon freshly squeezed lemon juice

fine sea salt and freshly ground black pepper

To serve

6–12 slices streaky bacon

leaves from a small bunch of flat leaf parsley, half chopped, the rest left whole

Serves 6

sautéed lentils with mushrooms
lentejas salteadas con setas

Put the lentils in a saucepan, cover with 1 litre cold water and bring to the boil. Lower the heat and simmer for about 35 minutes or until tender (the time will depend on the age of the lentils). Drain.

Heat 2 tablespoons of the oil in a frying pan, add the onion and garlic and fry for about 10 minutes until soft and pale golden. Add the butter, the remaining oil and the mushrooms. Stir-fry until the mushrooms are just cooked. Add the lentils, chopped parsley, lemon juice, salt and pepper and continue to stir until heated through.

Meanwhile, grill the bacon until crisp. Serve the lentils topped with the parsley and 1–2 slices of bacon per serving.

Variations To make 2 other classic lentil dishes:
• Add 150 g cubed Spanish panceta instead of the mushrooms.
• Add 4 skinned, deseeded, chopped tomatoes instead of the mushrooms.

Choose onions about the size of shallots, but not quite as small as pickling onions. A fast way to peel them and to keep a nice shape is to put them in a bowl or saucepan, cover with boiling water, drain, then rinse in cold water – the skins just fall off.

Braising is an excellent way to cook small onions. In Spain, large yellow onions are very sweet and are often eaten raw after being soaked in water for a little while – a habit that is said to go back to the Moors.

braised onions
cebollas guisadas

750 g small onions

4 tablespoons olive oil

4 garlic cloves, peeled and halved lengthways

a sprig of bay leaves

1 teaspoon smoked sweet paprika (pimentón dulce)

4 tablespoons dry white wine

coarse sea salt and freshly ground black pepper

Serves 4

Peel the onions, but leave the root end on.

Heat the oil in a heavy or cast iron enamelled heatproof casserole with a lid. Add the onions, garlic and bay leaves and cook over medium heat for 5 minutes. Stir often to stop them browning.

Add the paprika, salt, pepper and wine, cover and cook slowly until just tender, about 25 minutes (however, they can take up to 45 minutes depending on size).

Potatoes were introduced from the New World in the early 16th century, and now are more of a staple in the Spanish kitchen than almost any other ingredient. They are usually either fried in oil until crisp or cooked in stock, so this recipe is a combination of the two methods.

potatoes in shirts
patatas en camisa

500 g potatoes

a pinch of saffron threads

2 eggs

1 tablespoon milk

70 g plain flour, seasoned with salt and pepper

1 large onion, finely chopped

2 tablespoons chopped flat leaf parsley

250 ml hot clear chicken stock

coarse sea salt and freshly ground black pepper

pure olive oil, for deep-frying, plus 2 tablespoons for shallow-frying

an electric deep-fryer (optional)

Serves 4

Cut the potatoes into 1 cm slices and put in a bowl of cold water to stop them discolouring.

Using a mortar and pestle, crush the saffron with a little salt. Put in a bowl with the eggs, milk, salt and pepper and whisk well.

Drain the potato slices, pat dry with kitchen paper, then dip them first in the seasoned flour, then in the egg mixture.

Fill a saucepan or deep-fryer one-third full with the oil, or to the manufacturer's recommended level. Heat to 180°C (350°F).

Fry the potatoes, a batch at a time, until golden – they don't have to cook through. Remove and drain on kitchen paper.

Meanwhile heat the 2 tablespoons oil in a frying pan, add the onion and fry until soft and pale golden. Transfer to an ovenproof casserole. Add the potatoes to the casserole, season with salt and pepper, sprinkle with half the parsley, then add the hot stock. Grind some extra pepper over the top and bake uncovered in a preheated oven at 200°C (400°F) Gas 6 until the potatoes are tender and the stock has been absorbed.

Sprinkle with the remaining parsley, then serve.

Pisto Manchego, from La Mancha in the heart of Spain, is probably based on an earlier Moorish aubergine dish. The original didn't include tomatoes or peppers, because these weren't introduced from the New World until the 16th century, after the expulsion of the Moors. This dish is very good eaten cold. However, I also like it served warm with a hot poached egg on top, or with a plate of Spanish fries (page 99) or fried bread. Both accompaniments are particularly good when cooked in good Spanish olive oil.

vegetable sauté
pisto manchego

150 ml extra virgin olive oil

2 onions, chopped

4 garlic cloves, finely chopped

½ teaspoon cumin seeds

2 medium aubergines, chopped into 1 cm cubes

6 tomatoes, skinned, deseeded and chopped, with the juices reserved

300 g courgettes, cut into 1 cm cubes

3 large roasted red peppers from a jar, cut into 1 cm cubes

1 tablespoon coarsely chopped fresh oregano, plus extra leaves to serve

2 teaspoons sherry vinegar or red wine vinegar

sea salt and freshly ground black pepper

Serves 4–6

Heat half the oil in a heavy saucepan, add the onions and garlic and fry over medium heat for 5 minutes until softened. Remove to a bowl. Increase the heat, add the remaining oil, cumin and aubergines, stir until they take up the oil and soften slightly, then add the tomatoes and their juices. Simmer until the mixture starts to thicken.

Fold in the courgettes, peppers and chopped oregano, season with salt and pepper and simmer gently, uncovered, until soft. Fold in the vinegar and serve hot or cold with the oregano leaves sprinkled over.

Note Traditional versions of this recipe often cook the vegetables to form a thick sauce, but I prefer them to keep their shape.

The first young vegetables of spring are the stars of this *menestra* (stew) from the Basque country in north-west Spain. Use tiny potatoes, thin beans, asparagus, peas and little broad beans just large enough to swell their pods. If you grow your own garlic, include young green garlic shoots as well.

braised spring vegetables
menestra de verduras

24 tiny new potatoes

2 tablespoons olive oil

30 g salted butter

100 g baby onions, thinly sliced

2 garlic cloves, finely chopped

4 slices smoked streaky bacon, cut into small pieces

150 g thin green beans

200 g thin asparagus

250 g shelled broad beans (500 g before podding)

200 g shelled peas

coarse sea salt

Serves 6

Put the potatoes in a pan of boiling salted water, cook until soft, then drain.

Meanwhile, heat the oil and half the butter in a saucepan, add the onions and garlic, cover with a lid and cook until very soft but not coloured. Add the bacon and cook for 4 minutes. Turn off the heat and leave covered. Add the potatoes as soon as they are ready.

Put the beans in a saucepan of salted boiling water and cook for 2 minutes. Add the asparagus and cook for 1 minute. Add the broad beans and cook for 1 minute. Add the peas and cook for 1 more minute. (If the skins on the broad beans are too thick, cook them separately and pop them out of their skins.) Drain in a colander and refresh immediately under cold running water. This will stop them cooking further.

Meanwhile, put the saucepan with the potatoes over medium heat, add the remaining butter, the green vegetables and 2 tablespoons water. Mix gently and warm through with the lid on for a minute or so, then serve.

sweet things

postres

The Moorish original of horchata was made with pine nuts, seeds and chufas or tiger nuts (which aren't nuts, but a tuberous root) and used as a 'pick-me-up'. Almonds can also be used instead of tiger nuts, and the drink can be found freshly made in *horchaterías* and ice cream parlours, chilled and delicious on baking hot days. As early as the 16th century, snow was used to chill fruit drinks, so it was quite a labour-intensive luxury.

horchata
chilled almond drink

2 cups blanched almonds, coarsely chopped

3 tablespoons caster sugar

freshly squeezed juice of 1 lemon

extra crushed ice, to serve

ground cinnamon, for dusting

Serves 4

Put the almonds, sugar and 250 ml water in a blender and grind as finely as possible. Pour into a jug or bowl and add 625 ml boiling water. Set aside to infuse for several hours until completely cold. Strain through a fine-mesh nylon sieve into a jug or bowl, pressing the liquid through with the back of a ladle. Stir in the lemon juice and pour into a freezerproof container.

Freeze for about 1 hour until crystals start to form. Stir well and serve in tall glasses with extra crushed ice, if using, and a dusting of cinnamon.

iced lemon crush
granizado de limón

coarsely grated zest and freshly squeezed juice of 8 unwaxed lemons

200 g caster sugar

extra crushed ice (optional)

Serves 4

Put the zest and sugar in a saucepan with 250 ml cold water and bring to the boil for 5 minutes. Strain. Add 500 ml cold water and the lemon juice, pour into a freezerproof container and freeze for about 1 hour until ice crystals have formed around the edge. Break up with a fork and serve. Add extra crushed ice, if using.

Variation Coffee Ice or *Granizado de Café*

Put 200 g good-quality ground coffee in a heatproof bowl or cafetière, add 1 litre boiling water, then stir in 300 g sugar and the peeled zest from 1 unwaxed lemon. Let cool completely.

Strain through a fine-meshed sieve or push the plunger of the cafetière, pour into a freezerproof container and freeze and fork as in the previous recipe.

Fresh fruit is the favourite way to end a meal in Spain – either unadorned or with a little piece of cheese. However, these two puddings are simple and keep the freshness of the fruit intact. Oranges have been favourites in Spain since the Portuguese first introduced sweet ones from China, and bitter Sevilles, used for marmalade, were brought by Arab traders from India. Strawberries from the town of Aranjuez, south of Madrid, are of superb quality, and in summer a little 19th-century steam train brings them to the markets in the capital.

fresh orange juice with strawberries
zumo de naranja con fresas

4 Valencia or other sweet juicy oranges

400–500 g strawberries, cut in half if large

200 g wild strawberries
(frais de bois), if available

6 white sugar cubes, coarsely crushed

Serves 6

Squeeze the oranges and use some of the flesh that falls away as you juice, so it's nice and bitty.

Soak the strawberries in the orange juice in a serving bowl with a little of the sugar sprinkled over. Serve with the remaining sugar in a separate bowl.

spanish fruit salad
macedonia de frutas

about 1 kg mixed fresh fruit

sweet sherry, to taste

Serves 6

Cut melons into pieces, stone fruits such as apricots and peaches into wedges, and grapes or strawberries in half. Sprinkle over enough sweet sherry to flavour and moisten. Set aside for about 30 minutes to macerate, then serve.

The fig tree is as ancient to the landscape of Spain as the olive tree and both thrive in the hot, dry climate. The earliest variety is small, plump and black, fruiting in early summer, with other varieties continuing into late summer. Black figs have thick skins, green figs have thin skins. Whichever you choose for this dish, make sure they are fully ripe – squeeze them gently in the palm of your hand. When ripe, they should give slightly. A slightly split and dewy skin also denotes ripeness.

fig fritters
buñuelos de higos

140 g plain flour, plus a little for dusting

1 whole egg and 2 egg whites

200 ml white wine

finely grated zest of 1 unwaxed lemon

3 tablespoons caster sugar, plus extra for dusting

8 figs with stalks

sunflower oil, for deep–frying

an electric deep-fryer (optional)

Serves 4-8

Put the flour in a bowl, make a hollow in the centre and break in the whole egg. Add a little of the wine and gradually whisk in the flour from the edges so it doesn't go in all at once. Mix in the rest of the wine and lemon zest, cover with clingfilm and set aside for 1 hour.

Put the egg whites in a bowl and whisk until soft peaks form. Add the sugar a spoonful at a time, whisking to make a shiny meringue.

If the batter has thickened beyond thick cream stage, stir in a drop of water to loosen it a little. Fold in the meringue.

Fill a saucepan or deep-fryer one-third full with the oil, or to the manufacturer's recommended level. Heat the oil to 190°C (375°F).

Dust the figs with a little flour and dip them into the batter. Add the figs to the hot oil, in batches if necessary. When the batter turns crisp and golden, remove with a slotted spoon and drain on kitchen paper. Dust with caster sugar and serve while hot.

This classic Catalan dish has become famous all over Spain. It is similar to the French crème brûlée, but in Spain cornflour is usually added. It is served in small cazuelas designed to be filled right to the top so the surface can be burnt with a branding iron (*quemadoro*) that has been heated over a gas flame until smoking hot. This instantly caramelizes the sugared surface. In the absence of this handy tool, use a blowtorch – household grills aren't usually hot enough. If you visit Spain, a *quemadoro* makes an interesting gift for friends who love cooking.

catalan caramel cream
crema catalana

200 g caster sugar

4 teaspoons cornflour

6 large egg yolks

600 ml double cream

400 ml full cream milk

freshly grated zest from 1 unwaxed lemon

½ cinnamon stick

6 shallow 200 ml dishes or cazuelas,
10.5 cm diameter x 2.5 cm deep

a cook's blowtorch

Serves 6

Mix 150 g of the sugar and the cornflour in a bowl. Stir in the egg yolks until smooth, but do not whisk or the mixture will form a froth.

Put the cream, milk, lemon zest and cinnamon in a saucepan and heat gently until it just reaches boiling point. Pour onto the egg yolk mixture and stir well. Rinse out the pan and add the mixture. Stir over a low heat with a wooden spoon until it thickens enough to coat the spoon. Remove from the heat, leave to infuse for 30 minutes, then strain into a jug. Pour into the 6 dishes and chill for about 12 hours.

Sprinkle over the remaining sugar and caramelize the sugar with a blowtorch. As the caramel cools, it will harden. The dishes can be left for up to 1 hour, but don't put them in the refrigerator or the caramel may soften if left too long.

Note Traditional mini-cazuelas are made of terracotta, and widely available in kitchen shops, Spanish delis and by mail order (page 142).

A more delicious version of English eggy bread or American French toast, *torrija* is one of Spain's best-loved treats. It is a sweet bread fritter that is eaten for dessert or in *confiserías* (cake shops) as a snack with a *cale cortado* (coffee with a 'cut' of milk). Easter is the big time for torrijas, but you find them all year round. In Spain, you would use the everyday *pan de pueblo* – a long loaf with a crisp crust. At home, I use a baguette.

cinnamon toast with honey
torrijas con canela y miel

150 ml milk
1 vanilla pod, split lengthways
freshly grated zest of 1 unwaxed lemon
3 eggs, beaten
1 long baguette-style loaf, cut into 8 slices
60 ml moscatel wine
olive oil, for frying

To serve

90 ml clear honey
ground cinnamon, for dusting
5 sugar cubes, coarsely crushed

Serves 4–8

Put the milk in a saucepan with the vanilla pod and lemon zest and heat to just below boiling point. Remove the pan from the heat and let cool. When cool, beat in the eggs.

Strain the mixture into a flat dish large enough to take 2 slices of bread at a time. Put the slices of bread on a tray and sprinkle with the wine, just to moisten slightly.

Dip 2 slices of bread into the egg mixture and let soak for a few minutes. Heat the oil in a frying pan over medium heat, add the soaked bread and fry until golden brown on both sides, about 4 minutes. Drain on kitchen paper. Repeat until all are done.

Transfer to a large serving dish and spoon over the honey, sprinkle with cinnamon and sugar and either let soak for a few hours or eat while hot.

If eating them cold, add the sugar just before serving.

Named after the patron saint of Spain, this cake is common in Galicia, where there is a shrine to St James (Iago) in Santiago de Compostella. It is traditionally adorned with a stencil pattern of his sword using icing sugar. It is a flourless, butterless cake with whole almonds still in their skins, finely ground. You must use a coffee grinder or spice grinder – an ordinary food processor will not grind them finely enough. Alternatively, you can use ordinary ground almonds, but the flavour and colour will be different.

st james's cake
tarta de santiago

250 g whole almonds, with skins

6 large eggs, separated

200 g caster sugar

a large pinch of ground cinnamon

icing sugar, for dusting

butter, for greasing

fine sea salt

24 cm deep springform cake tin, greased with butter and base-lined (slash the paper so it reaches 3 cm up the sides)

Serves 8–12

Using a clean coffee grinder, grind the almonds until fine, with no lumps.

Put the egg whites and a pinch of salt in a bowl and whisk until soft peaks form. Whisk in half the sugar, 1 tablespoon at a time, to stabilize the whites.

Whisk the yolks with the remaining sugar and cinnamon until thick and the volume has increased. The mixture should leave a trail when you raise the whisk from the bowl.

Fold the ground almonds into the egg yolk mixture. Fold in a little of the whites to loosen the mixture, then fold in the remainder. Spoon into the tin and bake in a preheated oven at 180°C (350°F) Gas 4 for about 45 minutes until cooked, golden and firm but springy. Check after 35 minutes – if it is over-browning, cover with greaseproof paper and continue baking.

Remove from the oven and let cool in the tin on a wire rack for 10 minutes then unmould onto the rack to cool completely. Dust with icing sugar using a stencil of St James's sword if you wish.

Popular in Granada, the last stronghold of the Moors, who ruled Spain for 800 years until expelled by the Inquisition in the late 15th century. During that time, they influenced Spanish kitchens to a huge extent, not least by introducing almonds to the repertoire of ingredients. Interestingly, Christian nuns took over the confectionery business when the Moors were expelled from Granada.

Serve with a bowl of whipped cream, *nata montada*, for dipping, and a *café cortado* – coffee with just a 'cut' of milk.

moorish almond meringues
soplillos granadinos

3 egg whites

a pinch of sea salt

200 g caster sugar

finely grated zest of 1 unwaxed lemon

½ teaspoon pure vanilla bean paste (see note) or the scraped-out seeds of 1 vanilla pod

50 g toasted almond flakes, chopped into small pieces

whipped cream, to serve

a piping bag, fitted with a 2 cm plain nozzle

mini muffin cases (optional)

2 non-stick baking sheets

Makes about 36

Put the egg whites in a bowl with a pinch of salt and whisk just until firm peaks form. Add the sugar, 2 tablespoons at a time, whisking after each addition. Fold in the lemon zest, vanilla and almonds carefully so as not to lose volume.

Fill the piping bag with the mixture. Pipe the meringue either into double mini muffin cases set on the baking sheets or straight onto the baking sheets. Bake in a preheated oven at 120°C (250°F) Gas ½ for 30 minutes.

Increase the heat to 140°C (275°F) Gas 1 for a further 20 minutes. Remove from the oven, let cool on a wire rack and serve in their cases with a bowl of whipped cream. (Remove the outer muffin case before serving.)

Variation This mixture can be made into cookies or *almendrados*. Double the amount of almonds, and grind them to a fine powder in a spice grinder or coffee mill. Drop heaped teaspoons onto greased baking sheets and cook in a preheated oven at 140°C (275°F) Gas 1 for 15 minutes. They will be soft when they come out of the oven, but firm up when cold.

Note Vanilla paste is found in larger supermarkets, often in the gourmet food department. For mail order suppliers, see page 142. If you can't find it, use the seeds from 1 vanilla pod.

After a night of revelry doing what Spaniards do best (eating, drinking and talking), churros and hot chocolate at dawn is compulsory, ensuring a blissful sleep. The basic mixture is a flour and water dough, but I prefer this variation with egg and lemon zest, which makes the dough softer and easier to push through a piping bag. A churros maker or *churrera* is a perfect souvenir for the keen cook to take home from Spain. Inexpensive and very efficient, it is a fat plastic tube with a screw-down plunger and ridged nozzle.

A *chocolate a la taza* (cup of hot chocolate) for dunking churros must be thick – more like a sauce than a drink. The commercial chocolate made for the purpose has rice flour in it, which I prefer instead of the cornflour thickener used when people make churros at home.

a pinch of salt

finely grated rind of 1 unwaxed lemon

1 teaspoon sunflower oil, plus extra for deep-frying

140 g plain flour, sifted

1 egg, beaten with 1 tablespoon cold water

caster sugar, for dusting

Chocolate a la taza

250 g plain dark chocolate, about 50 per cent cocoa solids, broken into squares

2 tablespoons caster sugar

a stick of cinnamon

2 tablespoons fine rice flour

an electric deep-fryer (optional)

a strong piping bag fitted with a star nozzle, or a Spanish churros maker

a wide oiled spatula

Makes about 12: serves 4

churros with hot chocolate
churros con chocolate a la taza

To make the churros, put 250 ml cold water in a medium saucepan with the salt, lemon zest and 1 teaspoon oil. Bring to a fast boil, then add the flour all at once. Beat quickly with a wooden spoon to bring the mixture to a smooth paste, then leave for 5 minutes. Beat the egg mixture into the paste a little at a time until smooth and thick.

Fill a saucepan or deep-fryer one-third full with the oil, or to the manufacturer's recommended level. Heat to 190°C (375°F).

Working in batches if necessary, spoon the mixture into the piping bag. Pipe horseshoe shapes onto the oiled spatula, cutting the flow of dough at 15 cm intervals with a knife or scissors. Slide them into the oil and fry for about 4 minutes until a rich gold, drain on kitchen paper and dust with sugar, heaping it on top as well in true Spanish style.

To make the chocolate a la taza, put the chocolate, sugar and 800 ml cold water in a saucepan with the cinnamon stick and slowly melt the chocolate. Put the rice flour in small bowl, add 4 tablespoons cold water and mix until smooth. Blend it into the chocolate, mix well and bring just to the boil. If too thick, add a little water and reheat. Serve hot with the churros.

spanish shops, mail order and websites

Brindisa
www.brindisa.com
Brindisa at Borough Market
32 Borough Market,
London SE1 9AH
Tel/Fax: 020 7407 1036
Thurs 11–3, Fri 10–6, Sat 9–4
Brindisa at Exmouth Market
32 Exmouth Market,
Clerkenwell EC1R 4QE
Tel/Fax: 020 7713 1666
Mon–Fri 8–5
Tapas Brindisa at Borough Market
18–20 Southwark Street,
London SE1 1TJ
Tel: 020 7357 8880
All things Spanish, including beans and pulses, charcuterie, cheese, chocolate, fish, fruit, ham, honey, oils and vinegars, olives and encurtidos, rice and paella pans, seasonings and vegetables.

Cinco Quinas
32–34 Wilcox Road,
Vauxhall SW8 2UX
Tel: 020 7627 5250

The Cool Chile Company
P.O. Box 5702,
London W11 2GS
Tel: 0870 902 1145
Fax: 0870 162 3923
www.coolchile.co.uk
Unusual dried chillies, pastes and spices.

Delicioso
Unit 14, Tower Business Park,
Berinsfield, Oxon OX10 7LN
Tel: (0) 1865 340055
Mon–Fri 8.30–16.30
www.delicioso.co.uk
Mail order Spanish charcuterie, cheese, confectionery, conserves, honey, fruit, game products, herbs and spices, olive oil and vinegar, olives, paella kits and pans, salsas, vegetables, seafood, wine and sherry.

Food and Drink from Spain F.D.S.P. Ltd
6 Broad Court, Beechfield Road,
Alderley Edge, Cheshire SK9 7AU
Tel/Fax: 01625 590790
www.spanishhampers.co.uk
A wide variety of Spanish food and wine, including hams, sausages, olive oils, cheeses, honey, turrón and seafood.

Food Lovers' Fairs
www.foodloversfairs.com

R Garcia and Sons
248–250 Portobello Road,
London W11 1LL
Tel: 020 7221 6119
Hispanic products including oils, cheeses, cured meats and seafoods, spices and sweets.

Iberian Foods
C/Inmaculada Concepción 45,
Hacienda del Tomillar,
Arroyo de la Miel,
Malaga 29631, Espana
Tel: (34) 952 44 53 56
www.iberianfoods.co.uk
Mail order and on-line ordering. Information on oils and interesting page on how to slice whole jamón.

M Moen & Son
24 The Pavement,
Clapham Common SW4 0JA
Tel: 020 7622 1624
One of London's best butchers, with excellent deli attached – cheese counter, fresh vegetables and meats. Extensive range of Spanish products including morcilla and other sausages.

The National Association of Farmers Markets (NAFM)
Tel: 01225 787914
www.farmersmarkets.net

P De La Fuente
288 Portobello Road,
London W10 5TE
Tel: 020 8960 5687
All Spanish goods including cazuelas.

Peppers by Post
Sea Spring Farm,
West Bexington,
Dorchester, Dorset DT2 9DD
Tel: 01308 897892
Fax: 01308 897735
www.peppersbypost.biz
Fresh chillies in season: check the website for downloadable catalogue.

Products from Spain
89 Charlotte Street,
London W1T 4PX
Tel: 020 7580 2905

Rias Altas
97 Frampton Street,
St John's Wood NW8 8NA
Tel: 020 7262 4340
All Spanish goods including cazuelas.

Seasoned Pioneers
101 Summers Road, Brunswick
Business Park, Liverpool, L3 4BJ,
Freephone: 0800 0682348 (UK only)
Tel/Fax: 0151 709 9330
http://www.seasonedpioneers.co.uk/
Smoked paprika and organic Spanish saffron in foil sachets.

Selfridges
400 Oxford Street,
London W1A 1AB
Tel: 08708 377377
www.selfridges.co.uk
Wide range of deli goods, preserves, pickles, pasta, grains.

South Devon Chilli Farm
Martinhoe Cottage, West Alvington,
Kingsbridge, Devon TQ7 3PN
Tel: 01548 854368, 01548 550782
Fax: 08701 353888
www.southdevonchillifarm.co.uk
Fresh, dried or smoked chillies, seeds and plants and a directory of local farmers' markets.

The Spice Shop
1 Blenheim Crescent,
London W11 2EE
Tel: 020 7221 4448
www.thespiceshoponline.com
Herbs, spices, blends, grains, nuts, fruits.

La Tienda
www.tienda.com
A wonderful American site for Spanish products.

WINE AND SHERRY

Pedro Ximinez
www.pedroximenez.com
Spanish site for the great sherry producer.

www.reservaycata.com
An interesting Madrid-based website describing Spanish wines and grape varieties.

Philglas & Swiggot
21 Northcote Road,
Battersea SW11 1NG
Tel: 020 7924 4494
Fax: 020 7642 1308
64 Hill Rise, Richmond
Surrey TW10 6UB
Tel: 020 8332 6031
www.philglas-swiggot.co.uk
Wine Magazine's Small Independent Wine Merchants of the Year 2002, and London Independent Wine Merchants of the Year, 2003, 2004. Extensive list of sherry and wines from Spain. Subscribers' club.

index